"The German, the Turk and the Devil Made a Triple Alliance"
Harpoot Diaries, 1909-1917

Foreword by J. Michael Hagopian

Gomidas Institute
London

© 2016 Gomidas Institute

First Edition 2000
Second Edition 2016
ISBN 978-1-909382-30-5

All Rights Reserved

For further comments and inquiries please contact:
Gomidas Institute
42 Blythe Rd.
London W14 0HA
England
Emal: *info@gomidas.org*
Web: *www.gomidas.org*

Table of Contents

Introduction by J. Michael Hagopian	v
Diary entries from:	
1909	1
1910	1
1911	9
1912	17
1913	27
1914	31
1915	34
1916	70
1917	79
Appendix	83
Glossary	101

Illustrations:

Herbert and Tacy Atkinson with Henry and Alice	6
Opening of Annie Tracy Riggs Hospital, 1910	10
Harpoot in summer	15
Washing clothes in Lake Goljuk	15
Maria Jacobsen and Alice Atkinson, 1912	21
Harriet Atkinson and her doll	21
Group picture. Thanksgiving at American Consulate, 1913	28
Picnic for hospital staff and their families	32
American Hospital Compound, Mezreh, 1913	32
July 10th entry in diaries	45
Celebration of circumcision by Turkish family	47
Clinic at Lake Goljuk for Kurdish villagers	47
Patients arriving at the Hospital, Mezreh	51
The Atkinson house, Mezreh, 1914	51
Men's Ward at Hospital	59
Infirmary operating room, Harpoot	59
Dr. Herbert Atkinson and Turkish officials	69
Mrs. Atkinson and children after their return to the United States	81

By Way of a Foreword

As I write a foreword to Tacy Atkinson's diary I am mindful of the wealth of information we have allowed to slip away and be forgotten. We lost so much documentary material in those years of the Genocide, so many stories carried down the Euphrates, never to surface to reveal the true magnitude of the monumental crime against humanity committed in the mountains of eastern Turkey—once the heartland of historical Armenia. So many memories, letters, records and photographs were then left in the attics of descendants of genocide survivors, rain soaked, tattered, neglected and finally thrown away. So I write this foreword as a once reluctant participant in the preservation of the memory of my ancestors.

My father, known as Doctor Mikahil, was a well established physician and surgeon in Mezreh (Kharpert), in the Ottoman province of Mamouret-ul-Aziz, when Dr. Herbert and Mrs. Tacy Atkinson arrived there on August 22, 1902. My father was a bachelor then and on occasion was invited to dine with the Atkinsons. In later years in Fresno he often spoke of his foreign associates, but I did not then admit that these persons and their stories were of any particular significance.

It was by pure accident that I came to realize the immense historical significance of the Atkinson diary. As a documentary film maker, I was involved in *The Witnesses* project of the Armenian Film Foundation. We were attempting to piece together the story of the survivors of the 1915 Armenian Genocide. It was in essence detective work, investigating the events of the past, attempting to weave together a fragile fabric.

Although I had interviewed over 350 eye witnesses to the genocide of Armenians, I had overlooked two of the most important eye witnesses from Kharpert, the town of my birth: my father and Cavas Garabed Bedrosian. Long after both had passed away I confessed my grave error. I took up the phone sometime in 1991 and called Dr. Sarah Bedrosian in Fresno, California, the youngest child of Garabed Bedrosian. When Sarah opened her files and the reams of letters, documents, consular reports, and photographs poured out, I knew I could begin to reconstruct life in the town of my birth in 1915, and thus make a film on the last days of Kharpert. Sarah had a treasure trove. I asked her if any scholars knew about her private collection. She said, "no." Did any newspapers or authors know of her collection? Again "no."

I learned that Sarah's father, Garabed Bedrosian, whom I had known as an old friend of my parents in Fresno, and now a struggling farmer, had held the important position of body guard and translator to Leslie A. Davis, American consul in Kharpert. I asked Sarah if she had read Susan K. Blair's excellent volume on Leslie Davis' reports to the U.S. State Department, *The Slaughterhouse Province*, in which her father as "cavas," bodyguard, was mentioned. "Yes" she had, but Blair had never contacted her. I knew immediately that I was blazing a new trail of research. I sensed that I was on the verge of a discovery.

Dr. Bedrosian spoke of a niece, who had gone to a bible school in the mid west, who had a classmate, who in turn was the granddaughter of medical missionaries in Turkey. Her grandmother had written a diary about the Genocide. Her name was Tacy Atkinson. She had tried to keep the diary a secret from the Turkish authorities.

Sarah handed me a copy of a typed transcript. After reading it that afternoon I realized that here was one of the most important documents chronicling the deportation and death of Armenians in 1915. But where was the original diary?

After several years, I traced it to the small hamlet of Middleboro in southern Massachusetts. I found Harriet Atkinson Newcomb, the youngest of the three Atkinson children, but she did not have the diary. She had loaned it to an Armenian acquaintance to "restore." My mission was to get to the diary before it was tampered with. (I was aware of the historical value of such materials being compromised by otherwise well meaning individuals who "cleaned up," "rearranged" or reconditioned original materials. I finally located the diary in Providence, Rhode Island.

Who was Tacy Atkinson? Why did she write? What was her importance, if any, in the web of Armenian history? Why is there an inconsistency in her penmanship? Why are some of her letters slanted to the left and some to the right? Why did she hide her notebook, and why are portions of the diary meticulously crossed out by her own hand? And would we ever know what she tried to conceal?

Tacy Atkinson was born Tacy Adelia Wilkinson, in Salem, Nebraska, on July 3, 1870. Her parents of Scotch-Irish ancestry were wheat farmers. During the Civil War her father was a Southern sympathizer, her mother a Northern. The earliest Wilkinson in America was a clergyman named William who arrived in 1635. In England, the Wilkinsons had been iron masters. A John Wilkinson was called the "iron king." He was the first man to use coal instead of charcoal in smelting and the first to build an iron bridge.

For a time the Wilkinsons lived in Cumberland County in western Kentucky. Later they lived in Independence, Kansas, where Tacy attended high school. For a year she went to Park College in Missouri. Then, with some friends she went on a vacation to Oregon. She liked the state and took a job to teach the first grade. She graduated from Pacific University in Forest Grove in 1889. She was twenty-nine years of age.

At the age of thirty she developed a non-malignant breast tumor, and went to the Lane Hospital in San Francisco for surgery. At that time Herbert Atkinson was an intern at the Cooper Medical College, later named Stanford University. He saw Tacy the first time as she came out of the ether. She was thirty one years old when they married in San Rafael, California, on July 7, 1901.

Unlike Tacy Wilkinson, Dr. Herbert Atkinson's family had a long tradition in the Christian mission field. His maternal ancestry went back to 1640 when the Kidder family arrived in the New World. They settled in Massachusetts and owned land in Falmouth. His paternal grandmother was Sarah Salt sister of Sir Titus who was knighted by Queen Victoria for inventing alpaca-cloth. She married William Henry Atkinson and they came to America when their son was nineteen. He married Calista Hatch. They went to India in 1867 to serve as missionaries.

Their son, Dr. Herbert Atkinson, Tacy's husband, was born in India. He was educated at Grinnell College, Iowa, and received his medical degree from Cooper Medical College in San Francisco. He and Tacy had a short, productive life together of fifteen years.

Herbert and Tacy also decided to enter the Christian mission field. After spending five months in Paris to learn medical French, Dr. Atkinson worked with the famed physician, Dr. Fred D. Shepard in Aintab, Turkey to learn medical Turkish. Herbert and Tacy arrived in Kharpert in August, 1902. For the first seven years they lived in an apartment at Euphrates College. For a time they also lived in some rooms of the hospital. In 1913 they built their own house in Mezreh. Although Tacy had had no medical or religious training she readily joined her husband in his work. For instance, when the doctor examined a Moslem woman, Tacy stood on the same side of a blanket with the patient and felt the body and described the ailment to her husband on the other side.

The Atkinsons, as other missionaries before them, found the region of Kharpert an exhilarating place. The city was situated at a four thousand feet elevation, overlooking a fertile plain one thousand feet below. The twin city of Mezreh stood two miles away at the foot of the hill. The mighty Euphrates river flowed through the region irrigating the land and enriching the soil. The plain of Kharpert supported over three hundred and fifty villages, mostly inhabited by Armenians. They were engaged in agriculture and produced crops bearing cotton, wheat, sesame, cereal, melons, and grapes. There were many groves of mulberry trees, and silk worms were cultivated. Some manufacturing took place. Sheep and cattle raising was also important.

Prior to World War I there were at least 165,000 Armenians in the province of Mamouret-ul-Aziz. About 70,000 of them lived in 91 towns and villages around Kharpert. They had over 100 churches and 130 schools. Armenians constituted approximately half the entire population of Kharpert and its villages, alongside Turks and Kurds.

The region was surrounded by the snow capped Taurus Range that arose to a height of ten thousand feet. The legendary Tigris River had one of its sources at Lake

Goljuk, a day's walk from Kharpert. The missionaries often went there for their vacations. One summer Dr. Atkinson and my father went there for three-weeks camping. The climate of the Kharpert Plain was dry, with four distinct seasons. In the winter it snowed. In the summer there were dust storms, and the sunsets were very vivid. From their windows of the Euphrates College, on top of a hill, the Atkinsons could sense the enchantment of the place.

The first tour of duty in Kharpert for the Atkinsons lasted until August 19, 1908, six years marked by frequent illnesses on the part of Tacy. They returned to the United States and traveled coast to coast raising funds to build a new hospital in Mezreh, just two miles down the mountain at the base of Kharpert. Alice, their second child, was born in America. They returned to Kharpert on October 23, 1909.

The years between 1910 and 1915 were the best for Tacy. She had completely recovered from past ailments. She was healthy. She walked a great deal, gardened and was a good horse woman. The Atkinsons had become fluent in Armenian and Turkish. The Atkinson children knew Armenian better than English, though the parents insisted that they speak English around the dinner table. The children led a sheltered life, and their mother tried to shield them from what was happening to the Armenians.

Tacy had been writing a diary from the time of her marriage, having been greatly impressed by her mother-in-law, Calista Hatch Atkinson, who had kept a very methodical diary when she was a missionary in India.

Tacy Atkinson was a right hander, but when her arm was temporarily paralyzed during college she learned to write equally well with her left hand. This explains variations in the script. The words change their slant every time she changed the pen to the other hand.

She was an unusually keen observer of life about her. Because of her husband's position and prestige she had easy access to all levels of Turkish and Armenian society, from the Vali (governor) down to the deportees and refugees of 1915. She had a sense of time and place, and instinctively knew she was recording world shattering events for posterity. She was fearful that the Turkish authorities might lay hands on her journal. She wrote with great circumspection, yet forthrightly.

Once she crossed out a portion of her diary. Eighty five years later, with scientific advancements in digital technology, George Aghjayan of Worcester, Massachusetts was able to decipher for my film *Voices from the Lake—The Secret Genocide* what she had written. It was about Pastor Johannes Ehmann, the German missionary in Kharpert, and the complicity of his fatherland in the perpetration of atrocities. Another time she left out a most important event that happened in Kharpert in 1915. When she was reunited with her diary nine years later, she added her final entry in the margin: "1924, the story of this trip I did not dare write. They saw about 10,000 bodies."

During the summer and autumn of 1915 Dr. Herbert Atkinson immersed himself completely into the unfolding tragedy. He labored around the clock. Fatigued and despondent he caught the dreaded typhus disease from the refugees. My father was his physician. On his death bed Dr. Atkinson believed that God had sent him to Turkey just for the task he had performed. He ran his hand through Tacy's short hair and said, "I will die on Christmas. I have measured my strength. I have that much and no more." He died two days later. It was December 25, 1915.

During the next two years Tacy Atkinson became a tower of strength in the province of Mamouret-ul-Aziz. Dr. James L. Barton, head of the Board of Missions, wrote of her in 1918:

> Mrs. Atkinson remained at the post, took charge of the large, important hospital and assumed the responsibility of protecting the large number of Christians who had been gathered into the hospital, some as patients and others as nurses and attendants.
>
> Alone she faced the military commander of the district under whose direction thousands of helpless and innocent people had been put to death, and pleaded for mercy for her people.

After the United States entered the First World War in 1917, Tacy prepared to leave Turkey with her three children, in the company of Consul Leslie Davis, Henry Riggs, Dr. Ruth Parmelee, Isabelle Harley, Griselle McLaren and Myrtle Shane. The Turkish authorities pleaded with Mrs. Atkinson to remain, "having been won by her life and devotion."

She left behind her diary as the Government had decreed that nothing written was to be taken out of Turkey. Her eldest daughter, Alice, remembers that the diary was left in a locked trunk in the store room of their Kharpert home. Nine years later it came unopened to the United States. Dr. Atkinson's seals, in English and Turkish had not been broken.

All three Atkinson children led productive lives upon their return to the United States. However, the eldest, Henry, who was born on November 4, 1904 in Kharpert, and who served as a Presbyterian minister in Wildwood, New Jersey, died on June 1, 1934 at the early age of twenty-nine. He is survived by Dr. Herbert Atkinson, a physician and surgeon in Stevensville, Michigan and by a daughter, Mrs. Merrill Skinner. The youngest child, Harriet, was born on June 7, 1911, also in Kharpert. She attended the Westminster Choir College in Princeton, New Jersey. Later in life she taught music and voice. She died in Massachusetts on February 2, 1998 leaving no heirs. Harriet was the last person to possess the second part of her mother's diary. I visited her three times between 1993 and 1995 and corresponded with her until her death. It was in one of her shoe boxes that I accidentally found a picture of my parents seated at a garden picnic on the grounds of the Tracy Riggs Hospital. They were the only known survivors of the Genocide from a happy group of Armenians sitting under the mulberry trees that afternoon in the summer of 1914.

The middle child, Alice Calista, was born on October 31, 1908 in Santa Cruz, California, during the first Atkinson furlough. She received a degree in Christian Education from the Biblical Seminary of the University of New York. She served for many years along with her husband, the Reverend Dr. Paul Raymond Oliver Johnson, an ordained Presbyterian minister. She has two sons, Dr. Timothy Johnson, who is a retired professor of geography at Temple University and serves on the Grosvenor Council of the National Geographic Magazine; and Dr. Raymond Peter Johnson, a psychologist and former faculty member at the University of Illinois.

I interviewed Alice Johnson on July 18, 2000, in Waverly, Ohio. A very spry and alert individual at ninety two she is the family historian. She provided me with insights into the life of her parents. When I arrived in Waverly she had a gift waiting for me: a portion of a four hundred year old hanging from behind the altar. Other cut portions had been given to the descendants of the Atkinson clan. As she gave me the last remnant she said, "Now it is full circle, the hanging was given to my father by the Gregorian Church in Mezreh; now it comes back to the Armenians."

It is a strange coincidence of fate to write this foreword. I must have known Alice and her brother and sister sometime in Kharpert. We must have met and played on the grounds of the Tracy Riggs Hospital as our fathers were struggling day after day to save lives at the operating table inside. Now I find myself assisting to preserve her mother's observations of the Genocide when I have lost the testimony that my parents had to offer.

Tacy Atkinson's last twenty years in the United States were difficult ones, yet productive. From 1917 to 1937 she managed to provide a good home for her three children on a small pension from the Board of Missions, supplanted by taking in boarders. At times there were as many as eighteen of them and the Atkinson children had to sleep on the floor. Tacy did gardening which helped with their food supply. She never remarried, but Alice recalls that there were two promising opportunities.

As I review Tacy Atkinson's life in America during those last two decades, I find it a time of personal turmoil, a period of emotional and spiritual struggle. She was obsessed by her experience in Turkey. The genocide of Armenians weighed heavily upon her. She struggled with its meaning. How could such a horrendous thing happen on God's Good Earth? How could He allow it? Or, did He allow it? And for what reason? And for what sins the Armenians had committed? And why no punishment for the Turks?

These thoughts also affected her friend Cavass Garabed Bedrosian who lost his faith for a while; they affected my father, another man of God. And they affected Dr. Herbert Atkinson whose daughter Harriet claims that he was so distraught by the Genocide that "it just undid him completely."

After her return to America Tacy Atkinson incessantly talked with her friends about the massacres in Kharpert. She carried on a voluminous correspondence about her experiences, all of which has been lost because the letters were soiled or tattered and the family threw them away after she died. She criss-crossed the country giving speeches and raising funds for Armenian orphans. She could not forget the refugee camps, the long columns of deportees, the shrill calls at night driving the people out, the distant howls and gun shots....

The Armenian Genocide had affected her physical and emotional health. Yet she found time while living in Northfield, Massachusetts, to teach a course on the Book of Revelation in the Bible. She wrote a serious volume on the same subject, which was widely used. She prepared elaborate charts about the "end of days" to provide some meaning and understanding of God's plan and of man's inhumanity to man. And maybe an answer to what happened in Kharpert—and all Turkey—in 1915.

Tacy Adelia Atkinson died of heart ailment on December 1, 1937 in Philadelphia. She was buried at Cape May, New Jersey. She was sixty seven.

Tacy Adelia Atkinson left behind a document of unprecedented importance—a legacy of truthful reporting. She wrote forcefully, cogently and with lucidity. Tacy Atkinson's diary represents crucial evidence because she recorded events on a daily basis. She had no axes to grid and held no biases toward Turk, Kurd or Armenian. The accuracy of her observations are corroborated by other foreign residents of Kharpert, such as the Danish nurse Maria Jacobsen, who also kept a diary, and U.S. Consul Leslie A. Davis, who reported developments to the government of the United States.

Finally, after ten years of gathering information on Kharpert and the Atkinson family, I finally solved a mystery that had been puzzling me. Why did Tacy wait eight years to begin writing her diary when she had had the inspiration to write it after she first met her future mother-in-law?

In July, 2000, I called Alice Atkinson Johnson again. This time she revealed that she also had a part of her mother's diary. Her sister Harriet had always spoken of "the diary," as if there was only one. What had happened was that Tacy had given part one of the diary (1901 to 1909) to Alice and part two (1909 to 1917) to Harriet. Part two begins with the Atkinsons arriving in Kharpert, which I had mistaken as the start of the diary. Now it turns out that the 1909 arrival was the second time following a furlough in the United States.

J. Michael Hagopian
Armenian Film Foundation
Thousand Oaks, California
August 2000

Editorial Note

Tacy Atkinson's diary is reproduced here in its entirety, with all marginal notations placed in footnotes or in the main text. All editorial notes appear in brackets and are initialed by the present editor. This publication also includes some supplemental reports which were found inserted in these diaries, as well as a separate report which Tacy Atkinson wrote upon her return to the United States in 1917 on the destruction of Armenians (See Appendix).

In publishing these materials we have silently edited for punctuation and spelling errors, and made some stylistic changes, without compromising the intellectual integrity of the original diaries.

I would like to thank the Atkinson family for making these diaries available to us, as well as the late J. Michael Hagopian, a dear friend, for bringing these materials to our attention and writing a foreword. This work is part of the Gomidas Institute's ever expanding Armenian Genocide Documentation Series.

Ara Sarafian
Gomidas Institute
London, UK
August 2016

"The German, the Turk and the Devil Made a Triple Alliance"

Harpoot Diaries, 1909-1917

1909

October 23
  We arrived in Harpoot safe and sound but very tired, and went to the Carry's for a while until we could get settled.

October 31
  Alice's first birthday. She took her first steps alone and Aunt Min brought on the table a tiny cake with one little candle.

November 4
  Henry is five years old today. Aunt Min also has a cake for him with five candles. How happy he was. After supper some of the young people came in and we all played games that he would enjoy.

November 11
  We began housekeeping and found Sahag as a cook.

November 19
  Herbert started on a tour to Chunkoush.

December 12
  Herbert returned from his tour.

December 25
  Christmas. We entertained half the station for dinner and the Carry's the other half. Dinner at 2 o'clock. The tree was in the Browns's and was done mostly by Marie.

1910

January 1
  We received callers, about 200.

January 21
  Alice was taken sick with a bad diarrhoea and fever.

February 22
  Washington Party. Henry and I went.

March 8
  I was taken sick. Abortion.

March 10
  They operated on me removing the remains of abortion.

March 17
> Alice very sick again.

March 20
> Boy in hospital very sick with intussesception of the bowel.

March 27
> Boy died.

March 27
> Our Easter. Herbert led and Dr. Barnum dismissed us. It was his last meeting with us.

April 1
> Mr. Ward and Miss Catlin begin to take their meals with us.*

[Insert: Letter dated 2 April 1910]

Dear Friends,

I have thought I would give you a little glimpse into our little infirmary. You know we were not able to open the hospital this winter as it is not yet finished so we are getting on with the little place which we have used for the past three years. It only holds about sixteen beds and so you see we are cramped. In entering the building we pass the little office where the nurses give thirty or forty treatments a day to out patients. Then we enter the men's ward. We have no free beds in this ward. Not because we do not need them but because no one has given the money to support a free bed, but this does not mean that we have no free patients there for we often have men come who have no money to even pay for food and in that case we go around among the other members of our circle and find if any one has any charity money which he is willing to give for this patient. If nothing else we send his food from our own table and give hospital services free. In the men's ward this year there have been a constant change of patients for the most part, very few staying for any length of time. Though we have had a few very interesting patients. There is Bedros one of our own church members from a village who has needed an operation for a long time but could not pay for it. At last through the influence of our touring missionaries the money was raised for his hospital expenses. Doctor was almost afraid to operate on account of the condition of the man's health, aside from his special trouble but finally consented, but warned his friends that he might not live through it. When they were starting to the operating room they turned to me and said "Now you will help us with your prayers while we work won't you." For some days his life hung on a thread but God spared him and when he began to gain his strength he was

---

*. [Marginal note] Henry graduates from kindergarten.

one of the happiest men in the world. He would lie there and sing most of the time. One day when another man was very sick and delirious I went down there and as I entered the ward the most peculiar sound met my ears. I was frightened. I thought it was the delirious patient. No it was only Bedros singing. He left the hospital a well and happy man. How we wish poor Mustafa could have left as well. Mustafa was a Kurd from the Dersim mountain over in the region of Peri. His brothers a [?] fine looking fellow announced his arrival here at our door one day when Doctor was not at home. He said when I opened the door, "I know you and Doctor. I saw you in Peri two years ago." Then he told me he had brought his sick brother all the way two days journey to see if we could cure him. I told him he must wait till next morning to see the Doctor as he was away. The Doctor found it difficult to clearly diagnose his case but decided to operate any way in the hope that he might help him. He was willing to pay any reasonable price. The Kurds always have money. I suppose much of it they got by robbery. The man was suffering very much. But in operating they found an incurable cancer. The operation then gave much relief and poor Mustafa thought he was going to get well and would lie there and tell us how he longed to get out on the mountains with his gun. Of course we knew that though he would be better for a while he could never again go out with his gun so we tried to teach him the beautiful story of the love of Christ. He would say, "Yes I am glad to learn about your Jesus." But that is about all we could get him to say. At last the time came when the wound from the operation was well and we could do no more for him. He was better than when he came to us though not well and he had to know the truth that he could never be well again. It was a pretty hard thing to see the strong athletic young man give up to die. I hope the lessons about Jesus made it easier for him. When he was going another man in the bed near him was at the point of death and the wild Kurdish nature of this mountain robber showed itself in his stealing the shoes of the supposed to be dying. The man didn't die and was awfully angry when he found the Kurd had stolen his shoes.

The only death we have had this year was in the men's ward and a very pitiful death it was. A little boy from Peri. He was about twelve years old and without a single relative or friend in the world that we could learn of. He was in a very bad state from heart trouble and [?] disease. He was from Peri and has begged the money in the market there to hire a muleteer to bring him the two days journey to us. The muleteer brought him to our door and this time also the Doctor was away but I took in the situation at a glance. One need only to see him to know he could not live. I know that both his expenses in the hospital and his burial would be on us, and as we have no fund for that it is hard to take in one whom we can not help. But it was more than I could stand. The poor little fellow, so weak, he could hardly stand with his whole body out of shape from the disease and his lips bleeding from the wind and cold, clung to me and cried as if I were his last hope in the world. I told him to go to the hospital and asked the nurse if she could take him in, but no he refused to leave my side until I had written a note to her telling her to take in. I at last wrote the note but told her I had no money for him and asking for her if she had. The muleteer took him and without waiting for her to answer went and left him and as he could not be left to die in the streets we have to take him. During the few weeks that he lived he was a very happy grateful little patient winning the hearts of all. "There angels do always behold the face of the Father in heaven."

Let us look into the women's ward for a few minutes. The first bed we see when we enter has Mary Schuyler's sweet face above it. It is the free bed supported in memory of the dear girl whose picture hangs above it. This bed is never empty. One girl who has occupied it for some time is a very pretty refined girl not far from the age of the girl in the picture. Her name is Akabee and her case will prove hopeless in the end, though her life has been much prolonged and she may lie with very little suffering for some time in consequence of her help received here. She has not had the bed all the time as there are other as poor or poorer than she. Another occupant has been little Aghavni (Dove) a child whose mother is very poor and who has herself been in the hospital for some time. Aghavni is a very sweet patient little sufferer from a tubercular bone in her leg. She has given us much anxiety but we hope she will sometime be well. I went in today and found an old women nearly blind in that bed. I asked her trouble but all I could learn was "It hurts." One woman who has caused us a great deal of anxiety is a Turkish woman, wife of one of the wealthiest Turks in the city. She has been there for half the winter and may be there much longer. She has a tubercular foot and Doctor has taken out one bone and feared for a time he would have to amputate the foot but now he hopes to save it. Like all Turkish women she is very hysterical and sometime frightens her nurses needlessly but she has really suffered and we have all learned to love her. I went in when she was coming out of the anaesthetic when she had her operation, and when I saw how she clung to her husband and how he devoted himself to her. Her husband is so fond of her that I think one would hardly credit the tales one heard about the way Turks treat their wives to see him devote himself to her. It really did me good for we see all too little of that here. She has a little baby seven months old which she has had to wean. I think it would astonish some of the careful mothers at home to see that little thing without a tooth eat bread, meat, apples, pears and anything else that they give it. It makes me tremble for her but it seems to grow and thrive.

I should like to tell all of others but I fear I have written too much now so will not give any more now.

Yours most sincerely

Tacy W. Atkinson

April 22

Baron Malkon arrives from America.

April 29

Carrys and Miss Catlin start away and the new pastor Badv. Vostan and family arrive from Diarbekir. We give them a welcome, then we all walk out to the garden to see Leonard's grave.

May 1

Leonard's birthday.

May 16

Three years since little Leonard went to Heaven.

May 19

Dr. Barnum died.

May 26

Herbert's birthday. We remember it with a bouquet of flowers. He is 40 years old today.

June 14

We move to the garden.

June 16

In the afternoon Herbert starts; in the morning the babies and I go to town, we all eat lunch there together then we come home alone telling him goodbye. In half an hour he appeared at the garden with Alice's araba. I give him a drink of sherbet and then the animals are passing and he says goodbye. We watched and waved until he went out of sight around the mountain.

June 20

I went into town and found Baron Malkon sick. I begged that they allow Marie to come and nurse him.

June 24

Baron Malkon died at 3:00 a.m.

June 25

Baron Malkon's funeral 7:00 a.m. Baccalaureate Sermon 10. Dr. Barnum's memorial at 2:00.

June 28

Commencement.

Dr. and Mrs. Herbert and Tacy Atkinson
with Henry and Alice.

July 2

All the rest of the circle move to the garden.

July 3

My birthday.*

July 4

We celebrate here in our ivan. Consul came to dinner. Firecrackers chief feature of evening. Men and Henry celebrate in proper style.

July 7

Our wedding anniversary. The 9th. A quiet day.

July 8

The folks start to the lake.

July 10

Mariam came to see us.

July 22

We begin making mattresses. Pompish Mariam has gone.

July 26

The folks are coming back from the lake today. Henry went in the goel swimming. He swam a little with me holding his collar to keep his head up. Thermometer above 88.

July 31

It has been a hot week with the thermometer about 90 all the week. The consul moved up yesterday. Henry is really learning to swim. Alice seems better. She is learning to chatter a great deal. Five good letters came from Herbert all in one post on Wednesday. They had been written at different times but reached me all together. Friday I went to the market and spent the whole morning buying cloth for the mattresses. We have thirteen finished.

August 9

This is the day I had expected Herbert home but as yet he has not come. Henry has been sick autiontoxication. He has also a sore mouth. Sunday Mr. Colt spent the day at the garden. He has come to overlook the ground for the railroad.

August 13

At 1:00 a.m I was awakened by voices and someone at the door. It was Herbert and with him two Austrian students who were walking across the country and had

---

*. [Marginal note] Henry with Kookaboo.

met him at Chemishgazek. He and Pilibos had walked with them from there 12 hours. The two fellows were so footsore that it had taken them twenty-three hours to come the distance. I gave each of them a hospital doshek and they slept there staying with us over Sunday. Their feet were so sore they could not put on their shoes, so came down to breakfast barefooted. We were all glad to see Herbert come. Alice was taken sick the day before he came.

August 27

It was little Esther Ward's birthday, we were invited to her little party. When we came home we found Alice with a high fever. The next day, Sunday, Herbert had promised to go to a village to see a rich sick Turkish Bey. That night they would not let him come home. Alice's fever was 105. I sent our gardener for him. Then the Bey let him come. He reached home about 1 o'clock. Alice was very sick till September 1. Her fever left her.

September 12

We moved to Mezreh. Alice seemed to improve from the day we came. It was Ramazan, and we could not get hammals to bring out things only a few at a time. We had to live in camp style. Patients began to come in before we had the rooms cleaned for them. What a time we had. Work, work. The carpenters were here yet many things were still unfinished. At the end of a month we were partially settled and were ready for the dedication.* The service was to be at noon. By eleven o'clock such a crowd had come that we saw we could not have them in the ward as we had planned so we spread rugs out of the doors and seated the men and many of the women there while crowds of women occupied the upper balconies. There was such a crowd it was impossible to have the perfect quiet we wished for the service. There were many short talks and many kind things said. After it was over I began to serve tea in our dinning room. We must have served hundreds of cups, though hundreds went away without it because they could not get in.†

October 21

The official opening of the hospital was on Friday as that is the Moslem Sabbath. All officials were invited. The head of the religion was asked to offer prayer and although it was in such high Turkish with so much Arabic I could not understand it, yet those who could understand said that except for the omission of the name of Christ it was a most beautiful and sincere prayer. There were several addresses and music by the orchestra from the college and then the unveiling of the firman by the Vali. When the service was over, all were invited to look at the

---

*. [Marginal note] October 16.
†. [Marginal note and hair sample] Little Alice Edith Atkinson's hair given by Grandma.

building, and afterward they came to our rooms where they were served with coffee and candy. Of course there were no Turkish women invited but the nurses and I took our place and demanded the recognition of all, as of course we shall have to often meet these same Turks in the hospital. We were formally presented to the Vali and shook hands with him, where of course his own wife would not have been seen for any money.

November 24

This was Thanksgiving and as it was our turn to give the dinner we were very happy to have it here in our new home in the hospital. All our circle were here except Mr. Brown and Miss Pool who were away in the village touring. We had the usual turkey dinner and afterward games and weighing and measuring. Mrs. Margot stayed all night here and Miss Daniels and Mrs. Brown at the consulate so the others stayed as late as they wished. I decorated with autumn leaves.

December 14

Cold weather began at once but work went on. I had a little Christmas tree trimmed up in our sitting room and we invited the Consul over for dinner. After dinner we all hung up our stockings and then took turns lying down on the lounge and going to sleep while we stuffed each other's stockings. The children were tremendously happy but no one was allowed to peep into his stockings till next morning when we had a grand time opening them. After lunch we all went up to Harpoot, the children and I were to stay till Tuesday morning. In the evening was the regular Sunday evening prayer meeting which I especially enjoyed as I had not been in one since September.

December 26

Monday was to be the Christmas dinner and it was a delightful one at the Riggs home. After dinner we were all invited down to the young ladies house where a Christmas tree was prepared and we celebrated in proper style. Herbert stayed all night with us that night and next morning we all came home feeling that we had enjoyed our Christmas very much.

1911

January 1

We stayed at home and received a few callers but not very many.

January 24

Herbert got up at 5 o'clock and started in an araba to Auguntauk where Mr. Brown and Miss Poole were. Miss Poole having written that she was sick, the bitter

American missionaries and Ottoman officials at opening of Annie Tracy Riggs Hospital, 1910.

cold weather having begun January 16. He got her here in a hard storm at 4:00 p.m. She was weak and nervous and he found her to have bronchial pneumonia. She was quite sick for several days and then began to improve until she could get up and dress.

February 2

After lunch Herbert went to the door and was surprised to see Miss Poole half way up the stairs assisted by Miss Jacobsen. As she was wrapped in a blanket he did not see signs of distress until she reached the room. Then she almost fell gasping for breath. Then he saw heart failure and began to administer restoratives, the most powerful, but nothing gave relief and in less than an hour she was gone. Herbert went to Harpoot to take the sad news while we laid her out. Mary Riggs came down that night and Miss Catlin the next day. We three with Marie made, or rather covered the coffin with white, inside and out. Next morning at eight we had a short service here with Mr. Brown as leader. Mercury was 6 below 0 F. that day. Henry and I went in the araba with the Consul. There were two other arabas. The service in the city was at ten. She was laid beside Dr. Barnum on the hillside. We ate dinner at the Riggses and came back home.

February 6

A deep snow fell, quickly followed by others till the roads were blocked. Snowbound with no posts coming or going. Deaths from cold. Wood famine. The last post went January 24. Long days and nights of bitter cold. Storm after storm, snow after snow. Wolves, suffering, death.

March 2

It begins to moderate and the snow begins to go. It is not gone till the end of the month, when the posts begin to come; news comes of more money. Herbert went to the market and bought a lot of cloth for me to finish the supply of bedding.

In April patients begin to come in fast. I could get no one to run the sewing machine, but I got Elmas to come down from Harpoot to make yorgans and mattresses. The patients came in faster then we could provide for them. Sometimes three and four would be waiting at a time for me to make clothes for them.

May 1

Little Leonard's birthday. I have been working on the children's summer clothes.

May 16

Four years ago little Leonard left us. I have been working on tiny baby clothes for the one we are hoping for.

May 26

Herbert's birthday. I gave him a napkin ring and Henry a waste paper basket which he himself had helped to make. Alice gave him a bouquet of red roses.

May 31

I have finished all the work I want to do before I am sick but to make a little flannel petticoat for Alice for next winter. If I have more time I will do it tomorrow; if not it must wait till next winter. The boxes came yesterday and all my letters are answered. If I have more time I will write to my sister again. If I should not live through this, I want Henry to have my Bible, and Alice all my little pins and my set ring. If the baby should live, let it have my watch. If not, let Herbert do as he chooses with it and the wedding ring. I have nothing else of value except love, love, love. Harriet's hair [sample pinned to diary].

June 7

Wednesday 3:00 p.m Harriet Elizabeth Atkinson was born. She weighed 9 ¾ pounds without clothes and was 22 inches long. She was so fat she could scarcely open her eyes. Henry and Alice were wonderfully happy and kept coming in to kiss her. Alice was not at all jealous but seemed to take on a new dignity. She has always had many pet names. One night someone called her Little One. She said "I's not the little one, I's the big one." Once I heard Henry in most persuasive tones saying "Come on with me, dear little baby sister." She said, "Henry, Alice is not a baby, Alice is Alice Calista Atkinson." Henry said "Alright Alice Calista Atkinson come on." She said "Henry, Alice Calista Atkinson is not coming." Harriet has short brown hair but does not look at all like any of the rest, but in some way, I don't know how, she makes me think a great deal of little Leonard. I had a very hard time and am very slow in regaining my strength. Do not have enough milk for the baby and have cracked nipples

July 1

We moved to the garden today. Came in arabas. It was a big job getting ready as I could do so little and we were closing the hospital.

July 3

My birthday. Herbert and all the children remembered it and all made me very happy. Their little gifts were very sweet.

July 4

We had a very simple quiet celebration at Mrs. Brown's. Herbert, Henry and Alice slept out on the balcony under the stars. Henry drives Herbert to sleep every night with his questions on astronomy. The other night when I was dropping asleep he came in and called me and said, "Mother, is the moon really made of green cheese?" I said no and he asked if it were made from butter milk, and when I said no, he said "Well, I thought Father was fooling me," and he went back to call him to task only to find he had gone to sleep. He gave us one question like this; If a well has a hole in the bottom the water will leak out won't it? Yes, well if you dig a well through to the other side of the earth, it will have a hole in the bottom. Which side will the water leak out?

July 16

Sunday when we went to get lunch, Henry went to help me put it on the table. He climbed up on the cupboard shelves to get something and tipped the cupboard over spilling all the dishes out onto the tile floor and breaking most of them. He and Alice sat down and cried and I didn't know whether to laugh or cry. Herbert heard the noise and came running to the rescue. Just then Mr. Ward came in to lunch. He and Herbert gathered up the fragments.

July 17

Alice went up on the roof alone and came down alone and then came and told me about it. Then she went and tumbled into the ghul. Henry was there and pulled her out. It was the little ghul and not the big one.

July 19

Herbert came home looking more tired and discouraged than I have seen him for a long time. He told me that when they were trying to erect the windmill it fell when nearly up and broke the upper part of the tower.

July 31

Herbert cut Alice's hair, she looks like a different child.

August 11

My mother's birthday, she would be 71 if living. Windmill goes up for second time.

August 24

Herbert was sick all night. Henry stung by bee in the ear; his ear was swollen to twice its size, and his neck and face swollen until he was a ridiculous sight. Cholera has reached Mezreh.

August 25

English consul from Van came.

August 26

Quarantine between Mezreh and Harpoot. English consul came up here for dinner. Henry is learning to use the typewriter.

September 7

We moved from the garden today. We could only get a few hammals as it is Ramazan, but I got on the horse and took Harriet in my arms. We loaded the hagabes with necessary things and put them on the saddle, and Herbert put Alice on behind me with a foot in each side of the hagabes, and then he and Harry put the cat in a bag and walked and carried the cat. When we started down the mountain I was afraid to ride with the baby so I got off and put Henry in my place and they put the cat into the saddle bags and I carried the baby while Herbert held the children and led the horse. We reached the hospital at sundown. The nurses were there and had our rooms in order and supper cooked. The first thing we wanted to see was the windmill. And how nice the hospital looked with its fresh paint. We were glad to be here next morning for there was a very cold wind blowing.

September 12

The hospital was opened and patients began to come in. Our new hospital cook began work.

September 30

We all went out to Kervank to meet Miss Harley and Mr. Livengood. We took our lunch and had a picnic dinner.

October 31

Our little three year old had her birthday. Pearl Summer came and played all afternoon and at supper Alice had her little pink cake with its three little candles and was a very happy little girl.

November 4

Mr. Livengood and Miss Harley came down to celebrate Henry's seventh birthday. He had a nut cake and seven candles and felt himself quite a man.

November 11

We all went again to Kervank and had another picnic when the Consul and Miss Martoon came.

The city of Harpoot in summer. Euphrates College buildings at left. Mission work was centred here until the hospital was built in 1910 at the foot of the mountain just outside of Mezreh where the country government was located.

Washing clothes in lake Goljuk.
Mrs. Atkinson at the right in the water.

November 30

Thanksgiving at Mrs. Brown's. We took little Harriet Elizabeth and had a short consecration service for her at the beginning of the service. We had a turkey dinner and a very pleasant evening. Alice, Harriet and I stayed all night at the Riggs' and came down on the horse the next morning.

December 25

Christmas is to be in the hospital. Saturday things were in a stir. Herbert and Marie decorated the house and the tree. I engaged Herepsema for a few days to help with the cooking. Dinner was to be at two on Monday, so I cooked most of the dinner Saturday. We had three geese, I made the dressing and Herepsema did the roasting. Then we made apple sauce and all had a hand in the plum pudding. Then I made nut, orange and apple salad. I also made a nut cake for the evening. Marie and I had previously made a lot of candy. That Saturday night all was in shape. The consul came up and ate supper with us. Then we all took turns going to sleep while we stuffed stockings. This is the best part of Christmas. The children enjoy it so much. This year little Harriet's stocking was added to the list. Next day was to be a day of rest. In the morning we opened our stockings and enjoyed them tremendously. Herbert led the service in the hospital. Monday morning we were up early for there was lots to do. At the last minute I learned that the Browns and Margots were not coming, so my twenty people were only sixteen. Mary Riggs came and helped set the table and put presents on the tree. The dinner all turned out good. Pearl barley soup, roast goose, Swedish dressing, gravy, potatoes mashed, baked squash, apple sauce, plum jelly, pickles, salad, Christmas pudding with cream dressing, fruit, coffee a la Turk, candy. After dinner came an hour of quiet without lights, which we all enjoyed. Then the lamps and Christmas candles were lighted, and then we had prayers, some music and a little program; after which the presents were taken off the tree. It had been planned before that the adults* should each give and each receive three presents, and no more. It was quite enough. The little ones had more and were wild with delight. After the presents were finished we brought in cocoa and walnut cake. At nine it was discovered to be raining very hard so we persuaded the young ladies whose araba failed to come to stay all night.

---

*. [Page 14 of the original diaries is missing here and the entry up to January 25th is taken from the Atkinson family's typed copy.—Editor.]

1912

January 1

It was a quiet day with us, we made a few calls and received a few.

January 14

The native New Year, when they have their Christmas tree. We had about sixty people in the lower ward and each one received several presents; the patients and servants with the doctors and their families. The same tree that served for us served again for them and they were all very happy. I had made new dresses for all the girls.

The poughkeepsie box helped us out a lot in supplying the presents. When we had our Christmas dinner I had given the servants and nurses very much the same dinner as we had.

January 19

The native Christmas. We made about a dozen calls in Mezreh in the morning, and in the afternoon we went to Housenik and called. The Vartabedians invited us to come on the following week to a feast.

January 20

We went to a very big feast at the Vartabedians. Mr. Livengood and Miss Harley were there also.

January 25

Alice and Harriet are both sick with influenza.

February 12

Herbert began going to Harpoot to help Ward with the accounts.

February 14

Henry began going with Herbert to Harpoot to study in school.

February 17

I went to Harpoot and took lunch with the Margots. It was one of the stormiest days of the season. Henry begins to take French with Mrs. Margot.

February 25

I went to Harpoot in the evening with Herbert to the prayer meeting, leaving the babies with Anna Varj., who has been here since February 15th. I have been writing letters trying to catch up.

February 27

Sahag is preparing to plant potatoes.

March 26

Grandma's birthday. We wrote a little poem all together and sent it to her in the form of a little booklet. Harriet gets her first tooth.

To Grandma*

Just your baby Harriet sweet,
Thirty inches from head to feet,
Eight months old with dimpled cheek,
Half as tall as Grandma.

Just our little mischief dear,
Full of sunshine, full of cheer,
Here and there without a fear,
That's your Alice girlie.

Just our manly big boy strong,
Working, playing all day long,
Busy, active, full of song,
That's your "boy-joy" Henry.

Tacy busy serving others,
Advising, loving, friend of mothers,
Teaching, scolding, helping others,
By true love your daughter.

Doctor, good as can be found,
Lifts his light two hundred pounds,
As he makes his daily rounds,
That's your own boy Herbert.

Father, mother, baby too,
Henry, Alice, one too few,
Birthday love we send to you,
To our precious grandma.

This program was prepared by Henry for a farewell party for Miss Jacobsen before she left the end of March:

---

*. [Typed insert.]

Program for Miss Jacobsen's Party*
Eight songs:-
One by three girls.
Three by Siranoosh and Hovsanna.
Four by Hovsanna and Marta.
The Buster and his tag.
The candle on the table.
Three songs by Alice and Henry.
Drawing and the prophet, three times.
Pegs and rings.
Everybody choose a song or game.
And then a little cocoa and cookies.
Finish with prayers.

Miss Jacobsen left on March 29. The girls and Herbert went out to Khankeuy with her. They had a pouring rain all day. I stayed and kept the hospital.

March 31

Easter Sunday. We tried to make it a happy day for all.

[Letter dated 12 April, 1912]

Dear Friends,

I want to give you a few little glimpses into our hospital. Our Danish nurse has gone on her furlough but our six native nurses in their blue and white uniform go about their work with a quiet dignity and faithfulness that pleases us very much. Of course there is much that they do not know and therefore need a great deal of help and oversight from Doctor and me. Down in the men's ward an older nurse is in charge assisted by a younger. At present there are several interesting patients. First we see an Arab nearly as black as a Negro. His leg has been amputated above the knee. At first he looked so weak and sick that whenever I entered I always felt as if I must go and listen to see if he were breathing. Now he is nearly ready to go home. A little farther is another man with a leg amputated. This is an Armenian and the brightest happiest patient in the hospital. He never seems to grieve over the loss of his leg but rejoices that he is getting well. The morning after the operation he greeted me with a smile and an expression of gratitude that his poor old suffering leg was gone. Then comes a little boy with his lower jaw gone with gangrene. He is only five years old. He is a Kuzzlebash Kurd, a race said to be without a God. We do not know his language and so cannot talk as he is a dear little fellow and cannot speak Turkish but he tries to tell me of his trouble by putting his little finger up to the bandage.

---

*. [Typed insert.]

In the bed beside him is another little boy, a Turk from whom the Doctor has removed the upper jaw bone. Doctor described it to me as a terrible operation. His recovery was so quick and complete that his face was only slightly disfigured. And in the next bed is a man whose lower lip was removed for cancer and a new lip made by drawing over the skin from the side. A whole row of bad faces you see, yet all was cheer among them as all hoped to be well, but a man the other side motioned to as I went in the other day and said, "Hanum, I am dying" and what he said was true. Poor man was in such a state all over that we had known from the first there was no hope. I spoke to him a few words about his soul. Yes he was already waiting for Jesus to take him. Then I asked about his family. They were in a village, a wife and three children. Then I asked if he wanted to go home to die but he said no, it is better here where he can have good care. There are usually about fifteen in this ward and are mostly surgical.

In the women's ward there is rarely more than one or two empty beds. In this ward also there is a woman with an amputated leg. She barely had it off in time to save her life. She is a Turkish woman but a patient sufferer usually. One night I went in and heard her moaning and saying, "Why does it lie to me?" I asked her who had been lying to her, then she told me her leg was lying. She knew it was off and gone yet it seemed it there and was paining. I looked over at Sunduz. She was also asleep, poor little woman! Whenever she sees me she catones my hand and says "Oh what does the Doctor says now? Is there any hope that I will get well?" When it is a fight between life with death, it is hard but when it is a fight between life with health, or life and possibly a long life in a miserable condition, it is much harder. This is the fight this pretty sweet little Turkish woman is making. When she came in the doctor operated with a rather hopeless hope of curing her. The operation failed. Her husband a fine looking young fellow seems fond of her, but it is to be expected, if she is given as hopeless that he will turn her out and take another wife. Poor little thing! In a last desperate hope the Doctor operated again. He is keeping her quiet with opiates to give the wounds a chance to heal. Will it hold? He is doing all in his power and the rest we are leaving with God. We are hoping now that it will hold.

In a bed near by is a young Turkish girl. When she came in the girls gave her a bath as usual and put on her the hospital clothes. Then they tried to put alcohol on her hair to take out the vermin but she would not permit this and began to scream and fight. The nurse came into me for help. I found the girl sitting on the floor screaming and striking in all directions with hands and feet. I sent the nurse away and sat down beside her and began to ask her about her home: then I asked her to come into our rooms as my guest for a little while. I helped her to walk and she came. I interested her in many things and then I sat down with a bottle of alcohol and began to rub my hair asking her to hold the bottle and pour it on for me. And here I will say that I have found that an alcohol rub once in a week stops my hair from falling, so taking the rub at this

Maria Jacobsen and Alice on the hospital balcony, March 6th, 1912.

Harriet and her doll.

time was no sacrifice. When I finished she allowed me to rub her hair also. Then I took her back sweet and serene to the ward. I told her the nurses were my girls whom I loved and I wanted her to be nice with them. Since then she has been gentle and sweet as a lamb. We have also a little Armenian woman who has been for years a faithful member of the church in Harpoot. She had a slight stroke and came here, and a few days later she had a second stroke and now cannot move or speak but she does enjoy having us come and talk with her, and seems to be really happy. The most pitiful case we had this year is here now. A little girl five years old with hydrocephalus. Her head is as heavy as her body. Doctor has operated on her twice and thinks he has stopped the growth. Her head has shrunken some since the operation. She is going home today. This morning I gave her a little doll. It was touching to see her joy. She seems to have a fair amount of intelligence and a very sweet little smile. We have all learned to love her. We have had several hundred patients, these are only a few of those who are here now. One little Kurdish girl who has just gone was operated on for hare lips. She was like a little wild animal and as she was up and about after the first day, and as we could not speak Kurdish we had a time with her. Her favorite pass time was to go out and bring in the wet clothes off the clothes line. She would carefully fold them up and come and hand them in. In vain we tried to tell her to leave them out till they were dry. She would run away and when we were not looking would go and do it again. One great big strong young Armenian has such an abundance of strength and cheerfulness that we wonder now it happens that he can be sick at all. He had a sequestrum from his breast bone taken out but Doctor went right down to the large arteries above the heart. The next morning after the operation I found him sitting out in the sun on the front porch. I said, "Well aren't you sick enough to be in bed?" He said, "I will go if you wish" and he jumped up with such alacrity and started that I called him back and said, "No, if you feel like that stay out here in the sun and enjoy life!" They come and go constantly. The blind receive their sight, the lame walk, all sorts of diseases come. Some are cured and go home happy, but a few go to their reward. We try to heal their bodies and we try to bring their souls to the great Healer, and for those who must go we try to lessen the suffering, and to prepare them for the life beyond, we fail in much that we try to do. We lack many things that we need to work with, which money could give us, and we lack much of the spiritual power which more prayers could give us. Won't you help us!

Yours sincerely

Tacy W. Atkinson

April 17

The following is the first note I received from my small son Henry.* He was going to school in Harpoot. There was to be a concert to which he had taken tickets for himself and the nurse girls. He went to school and forgot them.

May 1

Little Leonard's birthday

May 16

Five years ago little Leonard left us to be with Jesus.

May 26

Herbert's birthday. Henry made the cake and arranged the presents we were all to give, except mine. I gave a water pitcher and then Herbert laughed at me and told me that on my birthday he would give me a revolver. He didn't though, but my little son gave me a package of firecrackers and then asked that he be allowed to shoot them off for me.

June 7

Harriet's birthday. Harriet was so happy with a new doll. Hajigul leaves us and I get Herepsema.

June 19

Herepsema announces her sudden engagement and leaves on two hours notice. We begin washing beds and preparing to close the hospital for the summer.

June 8

The Barnum-Riggs party arrive and we all go out to meet them.

June 11

Lorin Riggs was born.

June 15

Mrs. Shepard and Miss Bewer arrive from Aintap

June 29

We close the hospital after a desperate effort and a very strenuous day. I stood on the front porch and told the girls goodbye and felt so tired I did not want to see or think of them for months.

June 30

My own father's birthday. A quiet restful day.

---

*. [Not included here.]

July 3

My own birthday. The morning the children made me keep out of the dinning room until they had my presents arranged. It had all been planned by Henry boy and the presents were all things which he liked and thought of course I would. We all had a good laugh over the slate and ruler and the firecrackers. There wasn't a single thing that was what I would have wanted, but it all gave me just as much joy and more for it was all so full of love. We had planned a picnic at the garden so we got ready as early as we could and went on two horses. We were invited to lunch with the Riggses and in the evening for supper we put our lunch with theirs and had it served on the ivan in picnic style. At the end a beautiful coconut cake was put on at my place and a chocolate one at Ernest's for it was his birthday too. It was a hot day and we came home in the cool of the evening.

July 4

We spent the day packing to go to the lake. In the evening there was to be a grand celebration at the consulate. Of course we all went. The consul had a grand display of fireworks. The consulate was decorated with flags, and the military band played. Also the orchestra from the Germans played. All seemed to have a fine time.

July 5

After all sorts of difficulties in getting our katurjis we at last started with eight katurs. Mariam rode one with Alice, Hovsanna rode another, and Henry a third, while I had a horse with Harriet in my lap. He got off at 10:30 but Herbert did not start for another hour as he had to wait for his bed which was not finished.

It was a hot day. Soghamon brought the cows. We plodded along very slowly. Once Henry's katur began to jump with him. Henry jumped off and walked a long way. When Herbert overtook us Henry rode with him. We reached the lake at 5 o'clock. We were all tired but we had some very happy little girls. Alice said "Let's just stay here and let the girls and the patients take care of the hospital." Then she said, "Let's have my birthday here." Next day Alice, the little pale girl whom we had to coax to eat for two months, came to me in the middle of the morning and said, "Mother, Harriet and I are hungry."

July 6

In the night there came up a strong wind and as our beds were not entirely ready and the tent only partially pegged down we didn't sleep much. In the morning it was cold and cloudy. We spent the day fixing up camp. A hard wind made it very uncomfortable. No one ventured in the lake.

July 7

Our wedding anniversary and Sunday with a cold rain coming down. We shut ourselves in the tent. Herbert and I wrote letters and the children slept.

July 8

The rain stopped and the weather was a little milder. Herbert and I took a swim.

July 14

A warm day again and Sunday. We all went up to the top of the mountain and saw Herbert off to Harpoot where he was to stay till the following Thursday.

July 18

Herbert came and with him came Miss Catlin, Mr. Livengood and Toros.

July 24

We had a big time fishing. Caught nearly five-hundred. We thought them a thousand before they were cleaned.

July 25

The Consul, Miss Bewer, Miss Riggs, and Miss Harley came, also Kevork and Garabed.

August 1

Dr. Shepard and Florence came and were our guests for a week.

August 13

Harry Riggs came and he, Herbert, Henry and Mr. Livengood took food and blankets and at 4:00 o'clock crossed the lake and went a thousand feet up the mountain and camped.

August 14

They climbed to the top before sunrise. Some of the others climbed that day. At night when Alice saw Henry and Herbert's empty beds she said, "Mother where will father and Henry sleep?" I told her on Hazar Baba. She thought a minute and said, "Mother, is Hazar Baba soft?" I told her that when she woke in the morning they would be away up on top of the mountain. When she got up she said, "Mother are father and Henry up in the sky?" I said, "Why no, why do you ask?" She said "Hazar Baba sticks up into the sky."

August 21

Miss Martoon, Mr. Ward, Miss Harley and Miss Catlin went home.

August 24

Guljuk Day. Some of us want to go over. We now have four of the nurse girls here and they all want to go, so I gave up my place to them as the boatman refused to take more than ten. There were twelve who wanted to go even after Dr. Shepard, Herbert and I had dropped out. There was a south wind but no whitecaps so at last Mr. Livengood, Garabed and Miss Bewer said they would go in our little boat. In the big boat there were no Americans but Florence Shepard and Henry. The big boat crossed in an hour. I kept the spy glass on the little boat and they fell far behind. In an hour the wind was worse and the lake covered by white caps. A Kurd who had been watching from a high point came down and told us that they were in the middle of the lake but making no progress. Then we went up on the point with the glass and watched and we could see they were losing ground. I was badly frightened. We spent the whole morning watching them creep along, sometimes gaining a little and sometimes losing. At 1 o'clock we saw them reach the island. We then came down and ate our lunch. At half past seven they reached home. The fish boat towing the little boat. Then we learned that they had broken an oar and had had to fight their way across in that gale with one good oar and a stub. They were soaking wet when they reached the island. There they waited two hours till a boat came and took them off. They ate their lunch and dried their clothes.

August 25

Sunday. Miss Bewer is sick today from her wetting. We had a windy night last night and most of us are feeling ready to go home. We hope to go Tuesday.

August 27

We were up before dawn. Harriet sat up in her little bed and called out "Mother" and then "Faver" for the first time. We started by eight o'clock but were delayed a long time in loading the arabas and did not reach home until 3 o'clock.

August 29

We invited Dr. and Mrs. Shepard, Florence and Miss Bewer to dinner. Mrs. Shepard was not well and did not come.

August 30

Dr. Shepard held clinics in the hospital for two days.

September 20

We began going to Harpoot to pack the Carry things. We kept at it for two or three weeks.

October 31

Alice had Annie and Grandma Barnum and Aunt Emma and Uncle Harry. Mary Daniels had just started home and also the Consul. War had been declared.

November 4

Henry invited Uncle Ward, Aunt Dora and Miss Martoon down for his birthday.

November 29

Thanksgiving. We all had a fine time up at Mr. Earnest Riggs.

December 25

Christmas was at Mr. Harry Riggs and we went up and stayed over night. There was a fine dinner, a pretty tree and a jolly good time with plenty of Christmas cheer.

1913

January 1

Herbert and I went up to Harpoot in the afternoon and came back with the basket from Grandma.

March 15

Work began on our house.

March 21

A cold winter followed and I did not go up again for a long time, but now that there is a telephone I am not so alone.

May 1

Little Leonard's birthday and I went up to Harpoot.

May 2

The Consul and wife and our new nurse, Miss Margaret Campbell came. We all went out to meet them. It was a rainy day so we had our picnic dinner in a khan.

May 26

Herbert's 43rd birthday. We all planned a nice time and in the evening we had a consul and his wife up for dinner.

Thanksgiving at American Consulate, 1913

Back row: Henry Riggs, Herbert Atkinson, US Consul Masterson, George Knapp, Mr. Livengood.
Center row: Aunt Belle, Margaret Campbell, Tacy Atkinson, Grandma Barnum, Maria Jacobsen, Mary Riggs.
Front row: Dora Matoon, Alice, Aunt Emma, Annie, Alice Riggs (Mrs. Ernest Riggs) with Loren, Mrs. Masterson, Miss Petersen.
In front: Henry, Harriet.

June 7 was Harriet's birthday. We did not celebrate then but waited till the eleventh and had her's and Lorrin's together. We had the two Riggs families and Grandma Barnum down for dinner.

June 27

We graduated our first class of nurses. We had the exercises out by the side of the ward building. It was pronounced a great success. Running water was promised as a gift to the hospital by an Armenian.

June 30

We sent out the last of the patients and in the afternoon we served a picnic dinner in the chiftlik to all the medical staff and their wives. There were sixty seated at the table.

July 3

My birthday and the children and Miss Catlin who was there then and Aunt Margaret had some little gifts on my plate. It would have been a merry time but for the thought that in an hour Herbert would start on his journey to Van and afterward to Jerusalem. At eight o'clock he kissed us all goodbye. Alice, the little dear, ran and pulled a red rose out of mother's birthday bouquet and put it in his button hole. We were a tearful crowd as we watched him ride away.

July 4

In the evening we went to the consulate to the 4th. There was such a rough crowd that we did not enjoy it so much as the year before.

July 11

At eleven o'clock we started to the lake. It was a hot but uneventful trip and we reached the lake at five o'clock and found Mr. and Mrs. Riggs there to meet us.

July 18

Mr. and Mrs. Masterson joined us at the lake.

August 9

Miss Catlin and Miss Campbell came to the lake. The summer here has been quiet and restful but very uneventful. My chief interest has been letters from Herbert. Henry has learned to swim splendidly. Alice is trying to learn but has not succeeded yet.

August 24

The Riggses go home Tuesday. We stay a week longer. Alice is sick and Harriet was sick last week but is better now.

August 31

We are going home tomorrow. Last week Henry set out to see how far he could swim. He swam down parallel with the beach. Afterward Uncle Tay stepped it off on the beach and found he had swam 520 yards. That is more than a quarter of a mile. Mr. and Mrs. Riggs went home last Tuesday. Uncle Tay and the English consul came on Monday. The Consul is a fine swimmer and gives us all points on swimming.

September 8

Last Monday we came home from the lake September 1. We went to work at once cleaning up and we took in our first patient on Thursday, September 14. On Tuesday we went to call on the Vali's wife. Friday we had Thomas Eff. and the English Consul for dinner.

September 11

A telegram came from Herbert from Aintab saying he had left Aintab September 10 and will reach here September 18. I must send his horse to Malatia to meet him.

September 12

Margaret's birthday. I invited the young people from Harpoot, also the English Consul down to supper. Consul and Mrs. Masterson came up after supper for the ice cream and cake.

September 13

A letter from Jerusalem came enclosing a flower from the garden of Gethsemene.

September 18

Herbert came today. I did not expect him as I had received no telegram after Tavit's when he said he had not reached Malatia. Herbert did not know of Tavit's telegram, that is why he did not send.

September 20

We went to the garden and had dinner with the people there and then a station meeting.

September 29

We got Miss Catlin started for home after various difficulties. Miss Mattoon went with her.

October 5

Harriet and her papa and the kittens are having a play. The Van Theolags led the service here this morning.

October 25

This morning a little rain came so Alice, Harriet and I moved our beds in. We have been sleeping out since May. Henry, Herbert and Margaret are still sleeping out.

October 31

Alice's birthday, she is five years old. Annie came down to spend the day with her and the little Ehmann children came over for the afternoon.

November 1

We all went out to Khankeuy to meet Marie Jacobsen as she returns from her furlough in Denmark.

November 27

Thanksgiving at the consulate. It was awfully cold. We had two big fat turkeys and a fine time. Harriet and Alice were so tired when they came home that Harriet went to sleep while saying her prayers, and when Alice started to say hers, she said "Oh! Mother, please let me skip a little." A few nights before when Harriet was saying hers when she came to God bless her different friends she said, "Oh! Mother, that's all right. Amen."

December 7

This is our last day in the hospital rooms. D.V. Our new house is ready and tomorrow morning we begin moving.

December 8

We were busy for a week getting settled. How pretty our new rooms look, and how happy we are.

December 25

We got a pretty tree for Christmas. The Mastersons came up in the evening and hung up stockings with us. Christmas day we all went up to Grandma Barnum's for Christmas. Of course we all had a fine time.

December 31

I invited the station down for supper and afterward for prayer meeting.

1914

January 1

We opened our new house and invited all our native friends to come and see it. We had a great many callers and a very pleasant day. Mr. and Mrs. Vartabedian came and helped us entertain and stayed all night the following night.

The Hospital Compound, Mezreh, 1913. Atkinson house on the left and stable on the right.

Picnic for hospital staff and their families.

January 11

We were invited to the consulate for a turkey dinner. In the morning we had the worst blizzard I have seen in Turkey. It stopped before time to go. We had the women's ward full of typhus under the name of typhoid. It was hard to get Margaret to go and leave them.

January 12

In the evening at supper Margaret began having a hard chill beginning of typhus.

January 15

We moved Margaret up into the front hospital room.

January 31

Margaret's fever left her. For ten days we had feared death at any hour. I dropped everything, sent the children away from home and nursed her. Marie came down and nursed her at night.

March 8

We brought Margaret over to our guest room; she began to walk a little.

June 1

A new consul came and the Mastersons moved up into the two front rooms of the hospital. Mrs. Masterson is expecting confinement.

June 20

The Pierces and Parmelees arrived. We had all planned to go out to meet them, but that morning Mrs. Masterson was not well so that Margaret and I stayed at home.

June 23

Mrs. Masterson's baby was born after three nights and two days of labor.

July 3

My birthday and we are moving to the garden. It was a hard day. In the evening we had dinner with the Barnums, and Earnest and I had our birthday cakes.

July 4

The usual celebration at the garden. Margaret stayed at the hospital with the Mastersons. They tried to persuade her to go to the coast with them, but it was decided her health would not permit it.

July 15

Guests for annual meeting begin to arrive. My guests were the Smiths, Dr. Ussher, Neville and Dr. Hamilton, and Miss North and Miss McLaren. I enjoyed them all very much and also all of the meeting but found myself very tired at the end entertaining so many and attending all the meetings. We were altogether about fifty Americans of whom eleven were children. We shifted our visitors around for meals so that we saw something of all of them.

July 24

The Mastersons started to the coast. They started to take Lucia with them but only two hours out, the araba upset, Lucia was thrown out, and her leg was broken. Mariam went on with them instead.

July 29

Our last meeting which was a very sweet and impressive one.

July 31

We had another sweet service being all still here except Mr. Stapleton who had gone.

August 1

We started the majority of the our guests on their homeward way and within an hour were stunned by the news of the war and the mobilization of troops.

September 3

The military authorities have asked the use of the hospital for sick soldiers. Herbert gave them one ward. We at once moved down and when they got there we were ready for them. We bathed and put to bed twenty men before we went to bed, and then began a work which I have enjoyed very much, working for Moslems, and I have found them always ready to listen to the scriptures. I have heard many things from their lips that have rejoiced my heart.

1915

January 1

We began Red Cross work for soldiers today, and began to prepare for one-hundred soldiers.

January 14

Herbert came home from the market in a hard chill and was sick with a hard attack of influenza for two weeks. Dr. Topalian was then here as a patient. He took charge of the hospital and also looked after Herbert. The upper floor was filled with typhus and took all of Margaret's time so I gave all the time I could to the lower floor.

February 17

I came home from the hospital aching all over.

February 21

Spots came out of my body and I knew I had typhus. Marie had come down to help nurse. She nursed me at night and Lucia in the day time. I have some remembrance of being rubbed and of cold baths but nothing very definite. I remember when they cut my hair. After some time I remember they told me my fever had been gone some days and I was better, but I was still aching all over awfully. I was so glad when they let the children come in. It seemed they looked so pretty and sweet. They were not allowed to touch my bed or me for a long time, but they often made me visits. Miss Harley, the schools being closed, came down and stayed with them for some time while I was sick. After she left I kept them in my room a good deal; part of the time Lucia stayed downstairs with them. My eyes and tears were bad from the typhus also my brain seemed unable to think clearly.

March 26

I was awakened in the morning by dear little Harriet pulling at my cover and saying "This is Grandma's birthday." At this time I was sitting up several hours each day, and could walk across the room, but had not been out of the room. I sat up nearly all morning and wrote a letter to Grandma. This tired me a good deal and after dinner I went to bed intending to sleep a little. Lucia went downstairs. Suddenly I heard Harriet scream. I listened if Lucia would go but the screams continued. I jumped up and ran out in the hall. My ears being bad I could not locate her. It sounded as if she were in the attic. I thought she had been playing there and had pulled something heavy over on her. I tried to go up but could not. I am so thankful I could not, for had I gone I would have missed her and she would have been lost. I think it must have been the hand of God that held me back for I know that people when very weak can do such things when frightened. I then ran to the head of the stairs and called Lucia. She did not come, then I screamed two or three times as loud as I could. Then I saw Harriet in our bedroom door running toward me all in a bright blaze of fire. The whole front of her was on fire and the flame coming up around her face. The next I remember I was down on the floor with her smothering the fire. I was in my nightclothes and so had nothing to do it with but my hands. With my right hand I got hold of the little shawl that was on my shaved head. Just as the fire was out Henry and Lucia, who had heard my screams, rushed up. I sent Henry for Herbert who happened to be in the hospital. The poor little darling was burned under her chin from ear to ear, with the upper arm from the shoulder nearly the elbow was burned also, and another at her wrist, besides superficial burns. She had gone into Henry's room found a box of matches and had struck nearly all of them. One caught in her dress. She began to scream and tried to run to me but the door stuck and she could not open it, when she heard me scream she remembered to run to the other door. It was the most awful moment of my life when I saw her running to me all ablaze. I think I must have fallen when I tried to stoop over her, for we were both on the floor and both my knees were skinned and bruised. I did not know that I was burned for some minutes after Herbert came. Then I saw that the inside of my left hand and the thumb of the right was blistered. I did not know how my right had escaped till I saw the blackened condition of my shawl. I did not know I was frightened for a half an hour afterward when I began shaking and trembling in every muscle. I did not get over it for hours.

March 28

Harriet was sitting beside me one day when she turned around and said "Mother I am glad you saved me." This twitched my heart.

April 9

Our dear baby still requiring much care. It is two weeks since the accident. I've been trying today to get the bureau drawers and our bedrooms in order. I've piled up a tremendous pile of clothes for mending but my hands are still sore, though I can sew a little.

April 22

We went to the garden for a little rest. We went in a pyton and in the narrow rocky streets of the Harpoot market our horses began kicking and then ran away. I caught the children in my arms to keep them from being dashed out as we swayed and lurched. They did not run far and a dozen men were ready to help us out when they stopped. Herbert was near us on horseback.

April 23

Herbert was sick in Mezreh but did not let me know till he was well.

April 27

Grandma Barnum's eightieth birthday. She had been sick but today she insisted on putting on her silk dress and all the circle came to the garden for dinner. After dinner she came out to the lounge in the sitting room and there we all came in to see her, but no one stayed long.

April 26

Marie was taken sick with typhus.

April 28

I walked into the city with the children and from there we came home on horseback.

May 2

Several Professors were put in prison.

May 7

Margaret arrived from Diarbekir in a terrible nervous state after her experience there. Marie is delirious, approximately crazy. Screaming the whole time.

May 9

Grandma Barnum died quietly but suddenly.

May 21

Marie smiled this morning for the first time.

May 28

Telegram came from Smith in Diarbekir saying, "Riggs come. There is work."

May 29

Mr. Riggs started in the afternoon for Diarbekir and Herbert was taken sick with erysipelas. It started in his nose and spread all over his face. He was sick two weeks.

June 5

Saturday. Mr. Riggs returned from Diarbekir bringing Mrs. Smith with him. Report of massacres in the villages near Diarbekir and many exiles going from Diarbekir.

June 7

Early in the morning I heard violent ringing of telephone. It was Pierce in the city. He had stayed there overnight and a small boy came in from the garden and reported the garden surrounded by gendarmes and said they were searching the house. We could not ring up the garden so thought the wire was cut. Mr. Riggs had plugged the bell to keep it from ringing and so calling attention to it. The cause of it all was that Mr. Riggs and Mrs. Smith had been searched and they found on Mrs. Smith a telegraphic code, a thing harmless enough as it was prepared as a means of communication between herself and her husband. They probably searched Smith's house and found the same thing for we heard nothing from him for ten days, although the Consul was trying to find out about him. At the end of that time a telegram came from him asking for Mrs. Smith as they were to be sent out by the Government. We wanted to send one of our number with her but were refused, so we sent a Turkish kavass from the consulate. We learned afterward that the guard sent by the Government wanted to attack her purity but this kavass said, "You touch her and I shoot you or you shoot me." Smith had been a prisoner in his own house. He and Mrs. Smith were allowed to go. Well, when they had finished searching our friends at the garden they removed our telephone instruments out there and in the city, but did not touch ours here in Mezreh. On Saturday preceding this some bombs made by an Armenian druggist here were discovered and then began an accusation of all the Armenians and a search for bombs.

Previous to this a member of our teachers and Professors and others had been imprisoned. Now began tortures to make them confess to having bombs. Before this time all Armenians had been told to give up their arms and many had done so. Now they began to torture to make them tell where their arms are hidden. Keserik had been surrounded and searched for eight days, then Husenik.

June 8

In the evening of June 8 our pastor in Husenik sent word to us that they were being imprisoned, beaten and tortured till they could bear it no longer. He had seen our dear old Professor Nahigian beaten till he could bear it no longer.

June 9

News came that Harpoot was surrounded. They were beating, imprisoning and torturing. News came that Prof. Tenekedjian had been beaten dreadfully and had had his hair and beard pulled out one at a time. At noon a boy came to us saying that he had gone to the prison to take food to his father. His father had written on cigarette paper rolled into a tight roll, and slipped it into his antera, "Send poison enough for Prof. Bujicanian (a graduate from Edinburgh University), Prof. Luledjian (a graduate from Yale) and Firmanian, as they could not bear the torture." Early that morning little Dikran Vartabedian came telling us his father was in prison in Husenik and asking us to go to Mr. Ehmann the German missionary here and see if he could do something. Doctor was still sick so I went. He said he was going that day to a council of the government and would do what he could. He told me his every act was watched and he was afraid to go to the consulate even, as he was afraid he would lose what influence he had. When the request for poison came I sent to him again. I did not think it wise to go myself so I sent our washer woman. In the afternoon the Consul was here and we saw one of our ladies coming across the plain. The consul headed her off as she was on her way to the Germans. With her was Prof. Tenekedjian's wife saying that they were torturing the professor trying to make him implicate the Armenians in the hiding of arms. But of course he knew the Armenians to be innocent of such things and bore his torture. Some other prisoners afterward saw this poor man and said that he had been tortured till he no longer looked like a human being. The last seen or known of him, he was bound between two other prisoners (as he was too weak to walk) and dragged out onto the road supposedly going into exile. In the evening of this terrible day a cessation of searching and torturing was declared and the people were given another chance to give up their arms. This was to last for a week.

June 16

It did not cease but was lessened. During this time a number of men lost their minds and some others were taken into hospital for heart failure. One of our hospital girls was in the city. The house she was in was attacked by men pounding on the door and calling the girls to come out. Next day she and five other helpless girls' teachers from our girls school fled to us for refuge. Of course we took them in and various others till our house was full.

June 17

The city was again surrounded but this time no beating, no torturing but imprisoning all men and boys. Some fled to us for refuge of course but there was no such thing as hiding here. We sheltered Dr. Dingelian our treasurer for some days. At last the police came to the hospital searching for him. He was in our house eating his supper but the police not finding him in the hospital took one of our orderlies who happened to have the same name. This was Saturday night. The orderly was released and Dr. Dinglian started to his home. After he had gone we learned that the city was again surrounded. A terrible storm came and we were very anxious for him but somehow he reached home but was taken a few days later. On that evening Mr. Vartabedian was again taken and brought to Mezreh.

June 20

Again it was Sunday. I went to Husenik I found the streets filled with silent children but no men but Turkish Beys and gendarmes. The gendarmes stared after me and the Beys scowled. In a narrow street I met a gendarme who stared and even turned around and looked after me. I glanced back and saw him. I suddenly turned around, walked back to him and said, "How do you do, were you sick in our hospital last winter?" He was completely surprised. He caught his breath and stammered out "yes" which was a lie for I had never seen him before, but he was so scared he would have said yes to anything. "Well" I said, "I hope you are well now," and walked away and left him apparently paralysed. All the men in the place were in prison. That day a large body of prisoners were marched down from Harpoot to Mezreh prison. All the Kurdish prisoners were released to make room for them. From our upper back balcony we could make out the faces of men we knew and loved. One was Hovhannes Luledjian, a brother to Prof. Luledjian. It is the last we have ever seen of them.

June 23

In the morning we were stunned by the news that all the prisoners were quietly sent out bound in the night. Among them were many, in fact most of the leaders among the Armenians. Several groups had been sent out before. One lot were the soldiers who were working on the road. They were brought in and shut in the Red Konak for a day and night without food or water and then sent out. These men we feel certain were sent to their death. Various rumors have come back as to how they met their death but nothing authentic. About this time warnings from friendly Turks and Kurds were whispered to us that a massacre was planned within ten days and then within six, and then within three, and all was strangely quiet. Searching for arms and incriminating papers ceased but men were still being put in prison, whenever they were caught out on the street. Large bodies of Kurds were seen moving in various directions.

June 26

Then on Saturday June 26 the people were told that they were all to be exiled, and they were to be given five days to get ready. Many prisoners were released. They were told not to take more than twenty liras with them but the rest was to be deposited with the government. They were told first that these men who had gone were to be recalled, then they were told that they were to wait for their families. We asked permission for two or three of the missionaries to go with them. This was refused. We were allowed to buy things from them but not to store things. They were told they were to go to Ourfa. Then began buying their things and giving money to the poor, making knapsacks and filling them with bread and giving out. At first we wept till it seemed that in our lives we could never do anything again but weep. Then the horror of it began to settle on us. We find it impossible to weep. This past week the police have been selling their things at auction. The Moslems crowd in and the streets are crowded with men, women and boys carrying all sorts of household goods. They are buying things for almost nothing. Many things are brought here and dumped down saying, "If I never come back it is yours." One of the Professor's sons, a special friend of Henry's came in and said, "Henry, I am going into exile, here are my stamp collections, if I die they are yours." Poor Henry burst out crying and everyone in the room cried. Women came with five and six little children too little to walk and too heavy to carry, whose husbands are in prison or have been sent away, or who are dead, with no money for bread at home much less on the road. Our sympathies have been drawn upon till our senses are numb. We hear of massacres in Egin and Arabkir. Women come from Ichme and Habousi and tell that their men have been bound, taken out an hour into the mountain and killed. In Pertag there has been a massacre. On Thursday the first assignment of people started. We were surprised to find that the government gave them donkeys to go on. Our hearts were lightened but on Friday we saw a caravan of women and children come in with no men or boys above ten years.

The Consul, Henry and I went to the place where they were camped, and talked with them. They were some of the wealthiest families from Erzroum. They started twenty-seven days ago and were soon attacked by Kurds, robbed and stripped, and all the men and boys killed and many of the women, and children also, and their girls carried away. Their guards made a pretense at defending them and afterward stopped in a village and got clothes for them, for all were stripped, some entirely naked, but most of them were left with only one garment. They told me the guards had provided bread for them and had been kind. Poor things were ashamed to tell me the truth but they confessed it to others that the guards had been careful for all but their honor, but not for that.

July 3

My birthday. Today crowds have started. I went among the people telling them to dress the boys as girls and hide their money next to the skin. What an awful sight. People shoved out of their houses, the doors nailed, and they were piled into oxcarts or on donkeys and many on foot. Police and gendarmes armed, shoving them along. Yesterday a large crowd of women from Kughi arrived but no men. Their men were all killed or in prison and all their girls carried away. The daughter of Garabed the pastor at Kughi was taken by a Turkish Beg at Kervank. Also a large crowd of villagers from the Erzroum region. Some of their men are still living because when attacked they took to their legs, but they tell tales of terrible suffering. When leaving Erzroum they were told they were coming to Harpoot, but there seems to be no plan of letting them stop.

July 4

Today Mezreh has been quiet but Husenik has gone. We are working hard to save our hospital staff but do not know. Last Saturday night two doctors brought in a strangulated hernia. All the girls were weeping and could not work so I went into the operating room and brought in some of the Turkish orderlies who know nothing. They saw at a glance that they need to keep the hospital staff. We do not know what the end will be.

July 5

Yesteday afternoon Margaret, Miss Petersen and I went down with some medicines to the place where the exiles are camped. I have never seen such a sight. Thousands herded together mostly women and children but there were some men and boys also, but very few young girls. Sick lying everywhere. They pulled at us from every side begging for medicine and it seemed that almost every hand was feverish. They crowded and cried and begged till we could not distribute our medicine wisely. Oh such a mass of human suffering. One young little thing asked for soap to bathe her baby born two days ago. Her husband was killed on the way. Another came begging us to take her baby which was born the night before. These people were from Erzinjan and Erzroum. They had been on the road six weeks. They don't know where they are to go. Turkish men and officials were looking at the children, especially little girls and choosing the best looking ones, and we saw them one by one being led away to Turkish harems which means a life of slavery. We found among the crowd three of our own college boys sick. We asked permission to take them to our hospital but were refused. Such hopelessness was written on every face. They had been attacked by seven different bands of Kurds, robbed and killed. Many had died, many had been killed, practically all attractive girls had been carried away. Many children too little to walk had been left by the way to die. Many mothers had thrown their children into the river and many had jumped in themselves. And this fate is waiting our own dear people here.

July 6

Ross Abbey Pierce was born last night. Today at noon the order came for all our men to go; they all came in and said their goodbyes. Badv. Yaghoian was here. He prayed with them and they went. Oh how terrible it seemed for we know they were going to their death. That night they brought down a lot from Harpoot, among them Melkon Eff. In the night they emptied out the prisoners eight hundred in all. They bound them together in threes and took them out at midnight. They took them off and about noon the next day they took them into a valley and made them sit down. Then the yuz basha (captain) gave the order to fire. They fired and fired and they gave the order to use the bayonet. At this stage some of them broke their bands and ran away. They went to a village and told this story. The guards followed them and killed them there. The villagers brought the report here. In the crowd were Mr. Dingelian our assistant treasurer. Brn. Samuel Manugian, the pastor at Husenik, Hagop Eff. Janjigian and Melkon Eff. Luledjian our druggist from Harpoot and many others whom we know. But our own hospital workers were not among them. They were in the Red Konak and have not been sent yet. The Red Konak has been filled and emptied several times. The first time it was filled they kept the men there a day or two without food and water. They all probably met a similar fate to those first described. We have a very much more authentic report of the eight hundred just described but I dare not write it now.*

---

*. [Marginal note] America, April 27, 1924. Our authentic report was from our pharmacist Melkon Eff. He escaped and in the night reached us in the hospital. He told us about the scene described. We hid him for some days until we were afraid to keep him longer. We then dressed him like a Turkish woman and took him to a friendly Turk in Harpoot. From there he escaped to the Dersim. I have not heard from him since.

July 7

Herbert and I went this afternoon to the camp of the exiles from Erzroum and Erzingan. Herbert took quinine and diarrhoea tablets to give to the sick, but it was far short of what was needed; the diarrhoea seems to be doing the work that the Kurds failed to do. Where families start out together it seems that the Kurds do the work; killing the men, robbing the women, and carrying off the girls. Where the men are taken out from prison bound the gendarmes themselves do the work; the beating and torturing in prison seems to have stopped and a few of those who had been tortured have been released. One day when we were eating dinner, Doctor by mistake helped an extra plate. Just then there was a knock at the door and in came Prof. Luledjian. He is a graduate from Yale. He sat down and told us in quiet tones which carried the weight of truth the way he had been tortured. He was taken out in the night and beaten on the feet, hand and back, but the orders were not to touch his head. They pulled out his beard one hair at a time, and tried to pull his hair but he had just had it clipped and they could not get hold of it. He was beaten till almost insensible, then was thrown into a water closet. He heard them beating his brother Hovhannes in another room. The cries of those who were beaten were terrible to hear. After a while they took him out again and beat him. Then the Kaimakam (city mayor) came in and beat him with his own hands, striking him a blow in the face giving him a black eye. Then he called on all who loved their country or their religion to come and beat him. He then lost consciousness and he heard someone say he was dying. He had wanted to die before and he and Prof. Bujicanian had tried to strangle themselves but could not. Afterward he was taken out and put on a donkey and taken to the Red Crescent Hospital where he was kindly cared for.

July 8*

Herbert went to the garden and came down through the city as they were starting out from there with a crowd of old men and boys. Hagop Agha Bennayan and Bujicanian's father and such men as that. Some so old and feeble they could scarcely walk but they were forced along with the butt of muskets. Women and children crying and screaming filled the streets. They were beaten back with muskets. Herbert came all the way down just behind them. When he reached here his nerves had all gone to pieces, and he found it hard to pull himself together. But events follow so close one upon another that we do not recover from the shock of one horror till another is upon us.

---

*. [Marginal note] Melkon arrived.

July 9

Yesterday the people from Erzroum, about eight thousand souls were sent out. The Red Crescent took in the sick in large numbers, but we were not allowed to take them. We hear they are not cared for at all there, but that is probably because they are so many. A new crowd of about three thousand came in. The Erzroum women who came in first and are from a wealthy class are shut up as prisoners in the Hojah school building. Many of the girls have been carried off. We are not allowed to go near them. We have managed to see a few of them. One is the daughter of the Erzroum pastor. Mr. Riggs has some money for her but has not succeeded in getting it to her. There is no market any more and we have a hard time to get food for our patients. And now many others have come and sat down upon us, whom we must feed but cannot hope to save. Women beg to give us their children or their girls.

July 10

We have been going every day to the Red Konak and giving petitions to the Government trying to save our men. Yesterday I went myself to the commandant and begged for them. Out of the eight he gave me one. I suppose that one will be retaken. This afternoon the dellal went through the streets crying out that on Tuesday every Armenian is to go without exception. [Among the Turks and Armenians both it seems pretty well know this thing is from the Germans. Even Mr. Ehman himself is coming to the conviction that it is the work of his own government. We all know such clear-cut, well planned, all well carried out work is not the method of the Turk. The German, the Turk and the devil made a triple alliance not to be equalled in the world for cold blooded hellishness.]*

July 11†

Today has not been like Sunday at all. Crowds are coming all day leaving their money with Doctor to be sent through later if they live to get anywhere. Women crying, begging us to keep their children or their daughters. We are forbidden by the Government to keep a single person. Women sometimes get angry and say "Do you want us to give them to the Turks?" Sahag's widow came with her four little ones, the youngest three weeks old. She wanted to give us the second one from the baby. Then she said she had tried to give all three to the Turks, but they would not take them. I don't wonder. Poor poor things, any one of their stories is enough to melt any true heart, but I suppose our senses can bear only so much, for

---

*. [This section in brackets was crossed out in the originals. —Editor.
†. [Marginal note] Our poor men went out last night from the Red Konak. Also the crowd of old men from Harpoot. Yesterday I went to the commandant myself and begged for our men. I made a special plea for Suren and it was granted.

50

Above. Facimile page of July 10th entry, including passage crossed out.

Below. Section crossed out in July 10th entry.

exception. Among the Turks and Armenians both it seems to be pretty well known that this thing is from the Germans. Even Mr. Ehman himself is coming to the conviction that it is the work of his own government. We all know that such clear cut, well planned, and well carried out work is not the method of the Turk. The German the Turk and the devil make a triple alliance not to be equaled in the world, for cold blooded hellishness.

there comes a time when our minds become numb, for we turn from one to another, and thought and sympathy for one is forgotten in listening to another. We may never get out of here alive but I shall always feel glad I am here.

July 12

I made an early visit to Mr. Ehmann to enlist his aid on behalf of one of the "eight hundred" of which I dare not write. I got no help. Today there were rumors of our houses being searched or people hiding. In the afternoon Mardiros Eff. came to tell us he was to be free and remain here. He immediately decided to get married and save some poor girl from being carried to a harem. He could have his choice of any girl in the country. He chose his former sweetheart who had broken her engagement with him once.

July 13

We are urging Mardiros to marry quickly as we have a preacher here in the hospital as a patient. The Chief of Police came to the consulate to take the names of those exempt, and said he was coming here and to the Germans. We sent for the girl to come here early this morning but she hung back and he hung back and oh dear me! We were expecting the police to come any minute and shove them all out. We tried to bring them to a sense of danger but she wanted to be urged, I do not know yet if they will make it go. A large crowd of exiles went out but not so many as was expected.

July 14

At 10:00 this morning Mardiros was married. He came over here, Henry got up early and baked a cake, a luxury which we seldom have now, and at ten the nurse girls and patients; a few of them came over enough to fill the sitting room, and Henry played the wedding march on the Orphem. We all wore our everyday clothes. It was not a very joyful wedding. The bride herself wore a plain everyday dress. There is a rumor that Constantinople had fallen but we do not know if that is true or not.

July 15

Today large crowds have gone from the city. We are told that the people who started Tuesday were taken to Hulakueh only two hours distant. There the men were killed, the girls carried away, and the women robbed and left. All is quiet in Mezreh today. We do not know what is still coming. Large crowds of women and children are coming in today. I don't know where from and those who are here are dying as fast as they can, and are being thrown out unburied. Vultures that are usually so thick everywhere all are absent now. They are all out feasting on dead bodies. The women started out today were followed by a large crowd of Kurds and gendarmes.

Top. Celebration of circumcision of Turkish boy. Fayuk Muftie's son.
Bottom. Clinic at Lake Goljuk for Kurdish villagers.

July 16

A boy has arrived in Mezreh in a bad state nervously. As I understand it he was with a crowd of women and children from some village, I haven't heard what, who joined our prisoners who went out June 23. This crowd was seen at Kezin Khan by Kavass Ahmet. In the crowd was the Arachnort, the former Armenian police commissioner. Profs. Bujicanian, Tenekedjian and Vartabedian. A great number of the leading men. This boy says that in the gorge this side of Bakir Maden the men and women were all shot and the leading men had their heads cut off afterwards. Then the children of whom he was one were gathered up and brought back in arabas to Turkish homes. He escaped from the Turkish home and came here. His own mother was stripped and robbed and then shot. Hovhannes Luledjian was in this crowd. He says the valley smells so awful that one can hardly pass by now. I do not know how he knows this latter as he must have been brought back before the bodies began to smell. The Catholic Bishop with a few select men who were promised a safe journey with special privileges are said to have been killed in Kezin Khan or in that region. I do not know how this news came back, but it seems to be understood as a fact and not as a rumor.

July 18

Fairly quiet today but we expect that crowds will go out again on Monday or Tuesday. We have heard that a number of women who went out two weeks ago are back here prisoners in the Red Konak, among them the wives of some of the Fabricatorians, Digin Floritza Vorperian and Annaghul. I do not know how we can find out if this is true. The Government has opened up two orphanages here in Mezreh. I have not seen them but I am told they are awful. Just before noon we looked up at the road that passes above the hospital and saw people passing. We knew they were from Harpoot so we ran to see them. Many had passed before we reached them but I heard a voice call out in English, "Goodbye, Mrs. Atkinson." I said "Who are you?" She pulled the cloth off of her face. It was Zarouhi Varj. Benneyan. Then came her sister Anna Varj., and later Mariam Tashjian, all bent over and wrapped in rags. She had dressed herself in this way so that they would take her for an old woman and kill her instead of carrying her to a Turkish harem. The gendarmes shoved us back. I tried to rush by and speak to some of my friends but was rudely knocked by a gendarme who said "I'll kill you." I did not hear him or pay any attention. The others heard him. I said "I want to speak to that officer." By going to the officer I got near enough to shake hands with some. I had nothing to say to the officer so I just asked him to be kind to them. But I got to shake hands with some of the people.

July 19

The consul told us last night that he had gone to the camp ground just after the Erzroum exiles had been sent on. He said that about three hundred of dead and dying were left there on the ground. He said it was the most awful sight he had ever seen.

Very definite word has come from the party of forty or fifty who were given a special buyurlty from the government. They were promised safe conduct and were given special guards. The Catholic Bishop was in this, Dr. Artin Beg and a number of prominent people. They were taken out near Kezin Khan, one day's journey, tied and shot by the very guards who had been given for safe conduct. All were killed but three women. One of these women was brought to the home of the Mudir of Kervank. Her sister, who is an American citizen here, went to the Vali, got permission and brought her back and she tells the story. The Mudir of the Red Crescent called here today. He is one Turk who feels dreadful about these things. He has six hundred in his hospital of these poor exiles. His death rate daily is twenty-five. They will not give him workers to care for them. He said, "If I can give them bread and water and a little soup, it is all I can do." He is surely doing his best. He may be a Moslem but his name is truly written in the Lamb's Book of Life. He says that one and a half million of Armenians have been killed these last few weeks. But he says our government could never do this alone. It is the work of Germany and Austria.

Mugurditch Nazarian's family started. He had gone out with eight-hundred, his wife, five children, his old blind father and father's brother. One hour out his wife gave birth to a baby. It was left to die, the wife brought back to a Moslem home, and the five children sent on with the two old blind men.

July 22

We've had a shock today. This afternoon Rebeka Vartabedian walked in dressed in a black Turkish charshaf. She was followed by two Turkish officials, one whom Herbert knows as one of the worst men in the region. Herbert sent her upstairs where I was. I sent for Margaret and we began to try to get her story. The poor child is only thirteen but so large and well developed and so beautiful. She told us that she went within two hours of Diarbekir. Her two brothers were killed but the youngest was with her. She seemed afraid to speak and we had trouble to get anything out of her, but she told us that she was to marry this bad man and she was to go back to her own beautiful home and live, and he had promised to bring her mother back from Diarbekir. Then he came up and in a harsh voice ordered her downstairs and demanded from Herbert her property which she had left here for us to keep. Herbert said he could give it only to the mother but not to the girl or rather not to him. He talked loud and made threats then said he would take it to the government. I don't know what the end will be.*

July 27

Not many people have been sent out the last few days but all are filled with fear. Many are coming to us for refuge. We have been warned many times that if we take in too many they will come and clean them all out, but people come and will not take no for an answer. We tell them no and later find them here. We try to send out those who have no claim on us, but they go outside the walls and sit till night and back they come. Poor things have nowhere to go, what can we do? It is a terrible question and yet if we keep them we know that those who belong to us will also be sent. The Kaimakam in Harpoot takes bribes from people, then tells them to go and hide in the hospital. He told one woman to go and hide in the school in Harpoot, then he said, "No, not there for the Americans won't lie and they will find you there." Then he said "Go to the hospital, no one will ask for you there." Anna Dingelian has just been to me. A Kurdish Beg from Malatia who knew her father has just been to her. He told her frankly that he had been ordered by the Government to help with the killing. He told her of many who had been killed. But he told her he was saving pretty girls and those who had money. She is not pretty and has no money but he told her if they sent her out to telegraph to him and he would save her for her father's sake. He would also save her children and mother. He said she need not be a Moslem but he would teach her children to be Moslems. She knows she would have to work in the fields and probably marry a Kurd, but she said she would prefer that to being separated from her children and perhaps belonging to twenty men. If she could be near her children perhaps she could teach them enough of Christ to keep them till a time of deliverance. What a terrible choice for a bright talented educated woman.

July 29

Yesterday a crowd went from Harpoot. They only went out about as far as the fountain and stayed over night. This morning early they were attacked by a few Kurds, but mostly their own guards, shot and butchered with knives and hatchets. One boy of about fifteen escaped and started back. A Hojah met him, put him on his donkey and brought him into Mezreh, then sent him to us. He had six hatchet wounds on his head and a bullet wound in his back. Doctor thinks he will die. The fountain is only two hours out of Mezreh. Yesterday we learned that some of our men in the prison are in a bad state of mind. I went to see them. They were called out and I was permitted to talk and read and pray with them. They asked me to

---

*. [Marginal note] 1924 Rebeka is now living in Philadelphia, the mother of two boys by that man.

Patients arriving at the Hospital.

The Atkinson house, 1914. Dr. Atkinson directing *arabas* at front.

try to get permission for them for some of the missionaries to go into the prison where there are 250 Armenians and pray with them. We will try.

July 31

Yesterday afternoon we received into our hospital thirty wounded soldiers from Moush. According to their report, the fighting was six hours the other side of Moush. Yesterday afternoon we saw smoke over Morenik. In the evening two wounded zaptiahs came to us from there. We dressed their wounds but asked no questions. This morning I went to one and asked him how it happened. This is his story. The villagers had all been sent away from Morenik but some had escaped to the mountains. The houses were sealed. Then ten? men came back and made a hole and came into a house. Yesterday some of the zaptiahs went to open some of the houses to give them to the Turkish refugees from Van. When they opened this house the men fired on them killing one and wounding these two. Then they fired back killing some. Then they burned the house and all other houses in that quarter.

August 3

Doctor had four operations this afternoon but just as he was beginning the commandant came to visit the hospital with Nejib Bey. They went, and they began operating, when I saw Nejib Bey come with a number of police. I went to see what he wanted, he said he wanted to take the Armenians. I said, "Very well I will tell the doctor." I went to the operating room and found the doctor cutting off the leg of Yuz Bashi. I came back and said that I could not tell him for he would be much troubled and his hand would tremble and he could not finish the operation. I said they must wait so I had chairs brought, also one for myself. I sat down asking God to help me. Then I turned to Nejib Bey and told him how hard it was for us to deliver over to death all those in our care. I begged him to let them go to their homes and he take them from there. He said his order was from the commandant and he must obey. I said I would go to the commandant and he promised to wait my return. The commandant seemed lenient at first but said the Chief of Police was the one. Then I asked to see him and I had a tussle with the two. I sat down beside him and begged. He refused to let them go as he said they would all run away. At last I left him and met Nejib Bey on the way. He said he would go himself. When I got back I found the police ready to take all. Then I saw the Mudir coming and evidently he had been softened for he did not allow them to take the women and he sent back some of the men. They only took thirteen, one of whom has since been freed. So far only twenty have gone from us to death.

August 2

I went to see Maritza Vorperian. She told me her story. She started from here on the Saturday when the richest families went. One lieutenant rode beside her father's family all the way. At the river he told the Professor that there was danger for him but that if he would give Maritza, thirteen years old, he would try to save him. The Professor said, "No, I had rather die." She had beautiful hair so her mother cut it off, thinking he wouldn't want her, but he said "If you cut her hand off, still I want her." They reached Malatia after ten days. The men and women were separated and the women put into a building. Then Maritza's mother decided to give her in order to save the Professor and Mushegh. She and Maritza went and begged and the boy was given but the Professor was not. Then the men were taken out the other side of Malatia and killed. So the lieutenant told Maritza, and we have no reason to doubt it. Then all the women were robbed except Maritza's family. They were taken to the home of her grandmother. The other women were sent out. In a few days some of the girls were brought back. They told Martiza that the women were all killed. The lieutenant left Maritza there and came back to Mezreh to get permission to bring her. Then he went and brought her in an araba, but the government will not allow him to marry. He evidently cares for her honor. He has taken a house, put her in it, and keeps two Armenian women servants to take care of her. He comes only once a day to attend to her needs and do her marketing. He cannot get permission to marry her. I wish he could.*

August 4

I went in the evening to see our men who are in prison. I was not permitted to talk except in Turkish, a police was present. I promised to send them some things they had left at the hospital.

August 5

Last night I was awakened by guns. I counted six shots and then fourteen more. I sat up and saw something burning in Mezreh. This morning we learned it was the prison, where Toros was confined. They came to the room where he was to take the prisoners away. They refused to go and shut the door and held it. Then someone set fire to the bedding. When the smoke began to choke them, they ran out, and as they ran out they were shot. Toros was shot. Another report is that the men refused to come out and the police burned the room. The fire was put out and the rest of the prison did not burn. Early that morning our men patients were taken from the house and put in that prison. We thought they had been sent out, so did not send their food.

---

*. [Marginal note] 1924. Maritza is now with her uncle in Princeton, N.J. going to high school. A very pretty girl. The Turk never married her but kept her in purity.

August 7

Today I went to Harpoot with Ruth to try to get permission from the Kaimakam to take our pregnant women to the garden for confinement. He received us pleasantly and gave us permission, provided we get permission from here. We are trying, but I don't know...

August 8

This afternoon Pere Basil came in. He was among the prisoners who went from us. He had been freed. He brought us word of the condition of our prisoners. Robbed and selling their clothing to get bread. We are sending them food now. Forty wounded men from Moush came.

August 9

Today I took Pompish Yevnegay to the commandant with a letter from the Kaimakam trying to get permission for her to remain in safety. It was a dangerous trip. Twice the man with us was stopped by police. Once I heard a man who was passing say, "That also is an Armenian." I expected every minute to see her taken. We failed in our request. On our way we met a crowd from Husenik. I think there were three or four hundred, old, poor, sick, weak, lame, blind and little children. Behind came a band of forty men and about thirty little boys. Oh it was terrible, we stepped in a side street till they passed. They all made a rush for a fountain at the street corner but were beaten back. Many of them grabbed at me begging me to save them, among them Dolita. But a policeman took his stand beside me. He did not speak but I knew why he was there. We have had women, children and boys come to us bruised, hacked and bleeding. One little girl from Huiloo. She says that women were stripped, then laid two together and their heads cut off. She happened to be the under one and she escaped with a deep cut in the back of her neck and came here. These people I met were put into a church yard for over night. They can't go far. They will be killed close by.

August 10

Today the sky and air is filled with locusts.

August 11

Today is my own dear mother's birthday. If she were living she would be seventy-five. I had a long talk with one of our officers, an Arab. He had just come from Moush. He told me of the awful things he had seen. One house filled with Armenians, men and women and children, then straw piled around the house and slowly slowly they were burned to death, three hours in burning. Another crowd of men tied hand and foot and piled one upon another, then kerosene poured on them and they were burned. On the road as they were coming they saw, in one place two hundred, in another four hundred, in another five hundred people beside the road and on the road with their throats cut. And hundreds of women and children thrown into the water. One woman he saw nursing a young baby. She was stabbed through and through several times, the baby went on nursing. Later another man picked up the baby and ran a knife through it back to front. The man who told me this is a Moslem, but he says it is not in his religion to do such things. They are done by men without religion. He says God will not always be patient with such wickedness. He will surely punish.

August 12

Two Turkish soldiers who were sick here a long time last winter were sent to their home in Malatia on furlough. They have just returned to their regiment. They came to call on me. I asked them of conditions in Malatia. They said that multitudes of the people from Sivas, Amasia and all the northern cities had come to Malatia and four different crowds had gone from here, two from Mezreh, one from Harpoot and one from the villages. Many more than that have started, but we are surprised that even so many have reached there. In Malatia the men are separated from the women and taken out a little beyond and killed. Then the women are sent out and killed, but the girls are brought back. But none of the Malatia women or children had been sent and many of the men also have not been sent. Today is Bayram. This morning the hospital was visited by the commandant and about thirty leading officials. Pardon has come for all the Catholics, and there is a rumor that there is a general pardon, but we do not believe it. We think it only a trick to get the few remaining Armenians out of hiding.

August 13

I went today to call on the Vali's wife since it is Bayram. She received me very cordially.

August 18

A telegram has come from Aleppo from Mrs. Vartabedian and several others, so we know they reached there in safety. This morning a pardon has come for all Protestants. The Vali has returned from the Dersim. A man came from Diarbekir saying that Mariam Bagdasarian has married a Turk, and that Mr. Knapp arrived there sick from Bitlis. He was attended by this Turkish doctor and visited often by Pompish Mariam and Bdv. Hagop and about ten days ago died there. He was given a Christian burial in the Protestant cemetery by Bdv. Hagop. We are trying to learn more about it.

Last night sister Helena died. We went to her funeral this afternoon at five o'clock. Today two big Kurds came and brought letters from some of our dear ones who have escaped to their home. This afternoon Ruth and I went down to the Gregorian cemetery where we had heard there were a number of exiles from

Trebizond and that region. We found perhaps two thousand. The others had been sent out the night before. These were mostly sick who had been left because they cannot travel. The walls are high and the air bad. Sanitary conditions bad, the ground filthy, so that we had to pick our way, people in filthy rags being everywhere. They pulled at us like wild animals begging for food, or money to buy food. The government sends them food but it is not enough. There were Turkish grave diggers there. They dug a big grave perhaps ten feet square, as fast as the people died they put them in. When they put in one layer, then they put on it a layer of dirt, and then another layer of dead till it was full. I saw several such graves that had been filled. When I passed, they had just covered one layer. I saw an old women come with a body of a child, clamber down and put it in. A little later I passed again and saw another that had evidently been dropped in. I asked the grave diggers how many they buried a day. They said fifty or sixty. It seems the plan to keep them there till they all die. At night I was telling an Arab officer who is a patient here. He said, "And do the people themselves see the graves where they are to be buried?" I said "Yes." He said, "Oh! How terrible! God will punish our country for this sin."*

August 21

The Mutassarif from Moush arrived as a patient. He has a bad heart and will probably die. In the evening some wounded men arrived from Moush, among them one Russian prisoner, an officer. He speaks only Russian so we have a hard time to talk to him.

August 22

Another wounded Russian prisoner, an officer. The Turks treat them well. He speaks German and French so we can get along better.

August 25

The Mutassarif from Moush died last night, so this morning we had a funeral a la Turk. The Vali and commandant both came with a squad of police and soldiers. We hear that Italy has declared war on Turkey. We fear it may make more trouble here.

August 29

Mariam Bagdasarian and the Turkish doctor whom she says she has married, though he says she hasn't, came up here from Diarbekir. The doctor treated Mr. Knapp but refuses to give information. Mariam says he was found hiding Armenians in his house, was arrested, and sent under guard to Diarbekir. He arrived there sick and died two days later, but was heavily guarded and no one saw

---

*. [Marginal note] The report of Mr. Knapp's kind treatment was false.

him but his doctor. It was all a lie, according to her story, about her visiting him, also Bdv. Hagop and Pompish Mariam. Also about the Protestant funeral and the coffin. No one knows where or how he was buried. Mariam knows the cause of his death but will not tell us as she is afraid. The doctor said he died of typhus in two days, then he changed and said five days. Two days from typhus is impossible as we have seen it.

August 31

We have secured a house from the Government for the children of our workers. It has a nice garden and the children are happy. There will be about forty when they all get there. They have been here for two months and, to say the least, forty dirty little disobedient children in a hospital full of sick is an awful nuisance, and I for one was happy to get them out.

September 4

Yesterday Digin Nevart asked to go to Husenik to get some of her things stored there. She took the horses and servants of some of the officials. Yeksa, the nurse, went with her, also Harutune, the night nurse. He went without permission, no one knowing he was gone. Over there he just put on the cartridge belt and revolver and cap of the officers' servants; also Yeksa gave him a red crescent badge and he went into the market thinking to pass for a Turk. He was discovered and arrested at once and brought back here. Of course we were all angry when we saw what a foolish trick he had done in these days when life is so cheap. Herbert was not here. I asked Dr. Daud to go with him to the police and try to save him. He said no. Then I asked Chaoush. He said no. Then, although it was sundown, I said I would go myself and I told Chaoush he must go to take care of me. This he had to do. The police were very kind but said I must wait for the chief. I waited until it began to get dark and then I knew it was not proper for me to wait longer so I left Chaoush and asked one of the police to take me home. They refused to let him go. Next morning we sent again, they refused again. Then Herbert went and the Vali, as a special favor, let him go.

September 7

Last night Anna V. Dingelian and her two children, Annagul Kasanjian and several others came back. They had been rescued by Kurds and had gone no farther than Isoli. They stayed in a Kurdish village. Then, when pardon came for the Protestants, the Kurds brought them in an araba to the outside of Mezreh and they came alone to Miss Petersen's.

September 15

School began for the children and I am busy. The police Mudir has come back and trouble has begun again. There has been no trouble since he went away. A crowd came back from Malatia and some of them tried to get their property back and that started the police again. Annaghul Kasanjian came here for protection. We heard that Mushegh Vorperian had come back also. It became dangerous for him in Malatia and he ran away and came back here. He was in danger.

September 21

We brought Mushegh Vorperian here and put him to studying with Henry.

September 24

Consul* took a ride to Goljuk. He says that beginning one and a half hours from here he began seeing dead bodies, and all along every few yards, mostly women and children, many of them freshly killed and all naked. In the lake there were many and even at our camping place there were several washed up.

September 25

Just after dinner the police came and said they were going to take all the Armenians down to the police station and write them. They assured us that that was all but it is so easy for the Turk to lie, that we did not believe them. I said I was going with them and I told Henry to be ready to go if necessary. Margaret also walked out and said she was going, then Herbert said he was going too. Many of the Armenians disappeared and I do not know yet where they were for the police looked in attic and cellar and found no one hiding. After we had started they found Mushegh, and Henry came with him. Mushegh was one they were specially hunting as he was one who come back from Malatia. Henry went with his father to the police Mudir and told him they had taken his friend and he wanted him back. And so he sent a police with Henry and took him back. I then went into the Mudir's office and found Doctor there. He said that only those workers would be spared who had been with us when they had taken the Armenians before. I went to the police and asked why he had told me that lie saying they would all be given back. He protested he hadn't lied, but I said he had and asked him what he was going to do when he appeared before God. The other policemen sat and grinned at his embarrassment. Now I said, "If I should tell you one lie then you never would believe me again, would you?" He said, "No." Then I said, "Do you expect me to believe you if you come to the hospital again? Now," I said "I think you had better ask pardon" He grinned, got red and asked my pardon. All the names were written, some of them lied fearfully. I trembled for them. I spoke in English and told them if they lied so it would be impossible for us to do anything to save them. At last the Mudir himself came out and talked. He began to scold and said "If you are not sick why are you in the hospital?" I was standing near a little boy with an

---

*. [U.S. Consul Leslie Davis. —A.S.]

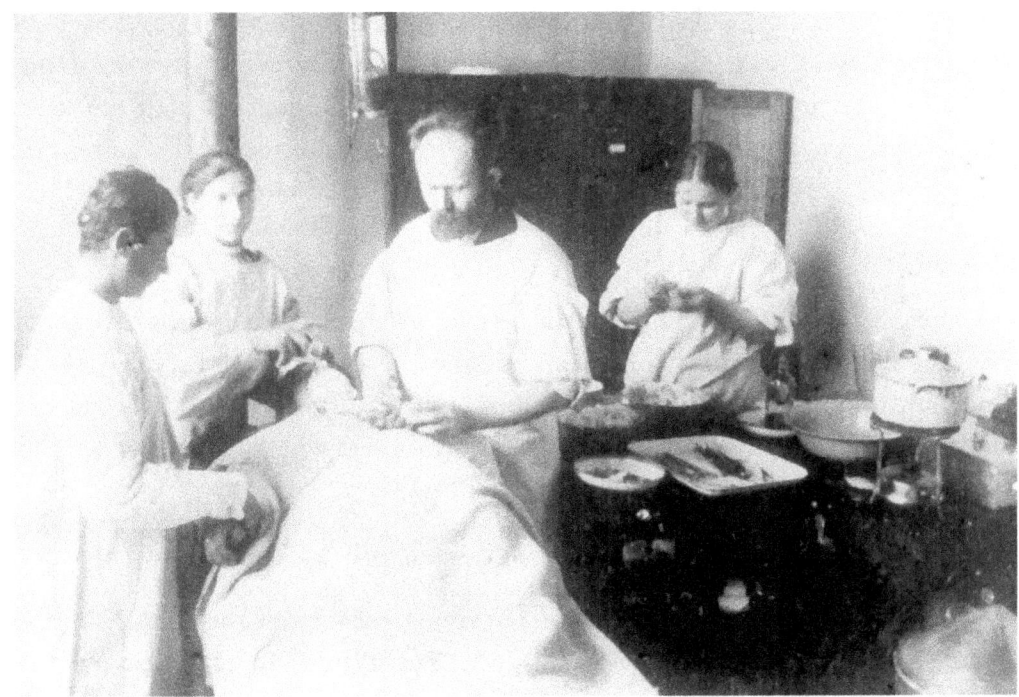

Top. Posed operation in Infirmary operating room, Harpoot.

Bottom. Men's Ward at Hospital, Mezreh.

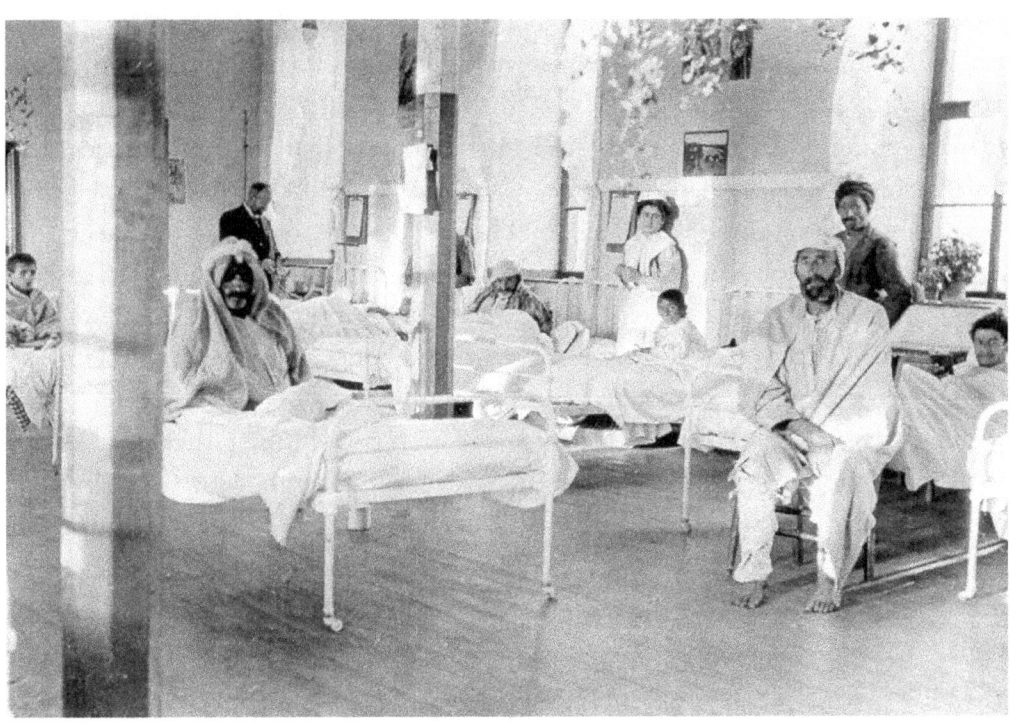

abscess on his neck. I jerked him around and pointed to his neck, and then to another sick, weak little fellow. Then he asked the men what work they were doing in the hospital and they answered. Then he said to me that we must not keep people who were neither workers nor sick. Then he dismissed us all and sent us home.

September 30

There is again much fear among the people. Several hundred Kurds have come from the Dersim, all armed and we do not know what it means. I received a call yesterday from the Vali's wife. She proposed to me that I promise her little Harriet for the wife of her little son when they are grown. I said when he is grown let him come and ask for her himself and see what she will say.

October 12

Marie came yesterday and called on me saying, "Have you any guests?" When I said, "No," she said, "Read that" handing me a card from Dr. Thom, saying that they were moving in our direction and would pass through here on Monday Oct. 11. What could it mean? Were they exiled? Had they been pushed through in the night without our knowledge? Herbert went at once to the Consul and they to the Vali. The latter denied any knowledge to them. Then Herbert came home, got on his horse and started out on the road to see if he could see him. It was well that he did for he had only gone a short distance when he met Mr. Andrus, Dr. Thom and Miss Fenenga, under guard, exiles from Mardin under what charge they did not know. Herbert talked with them all the way back to Mezreh. They were taken to a khan and when the guards woke up to the fact that he was a friend, they ordered him off, and when he went and told the Consul and they returned they were allowed to speak only in Turkish. The consul promised to go to see the Vali and try to get permission for them to spend the night in the consulate. In case he could not they promised to send them food. After supper Herbert and I went to the consulate. They were not there but word had come that we might go and see them. Herbert and I went and while we were there a police came and gave permission for them to come to the consulate for supper but said they must return to the khan for the night. The police went with them. Next morning Herbert went and brought them here for breakfast, the police occupying the best seat in our living room while they ate. Before we finished Emma and Harry came. Later others from Harpoot who all stayed for dinner. They were allowed after this to remain at the consulate and the Consul was busy trying to get a wire through to the ambassador but could get no reply.

October 16

The Mardin friends are told they must move on to Sivas inside of 24 hours. They have no idea as to the nature of their crime.

October 17

Sunday morning. We have to tell our Mardin friends goodbye as they start on to Malatia under three guards. Harriet said to me in the evening, "Mother are those people really exiles?" Think of a child four years old knowing what an exile is.

October 22

We have all been advised by ambassador Morgenthau to leave the country by way of Beirut.

October 23

We met to discuss the proposition of leaving the country. It was decided that only enough should remain to carry on relief work. We here at the hospital are to stay till we have to go and Henry and Emma Riggs are to stay also. Also Miss Harley and Miss Jacobsen. We do not know what it may mean to stay, it may mean the worst later on but at least we cannot desert the people.

October 24

Doctor and Consul started on a trip around the lake to see what they can see. It will be two days.*

October 31

Alice's birthday a very happy little girl. Her best birthday present was a little table and four chairs for school. I gave her a music book in which she's taking organ lessons. A cake with seven candles.

November 4

Henry's birthday. He had his share of presents and I gave the children all a holiday. I baked a chocolate cake for him. It was a beautiful warm day and his father took all three of them to the city in the afternoon and Karekin went along. I had a headache and lay down to rest a little while in the afternoon when Dolita came and told me the police had taken two of our boys. It took me some time to wake up, as the police had not sent anyone away for eight days, and it is forty days since we have been disturbed by them at all. I went out and found a police taking away some of our boys and some others also. I found a gendarme at each gate. They said their orders were not to let anyone go out or in. I at length got them to

---

*. [Marginal note] 1924. The story of this trip I did not dare to write. They saw about ten thousand bodies.

let me go and I went to the consulate. There I found a policeman on guard. He let me pass but refused to allow Armenians to pass. I went to the police station. I saw the police Mudir riding away at top speed. I went in and found a number of men, women and children already there. Among them several of our own people. I asked the head of police what it meant. He said he thought it meant nothing for the Syrians but that the Armenians would be sorted over and some would be freed and the others, he didn't know. I saw I could do nothing till the Mudir came so I started away. On my way I met a large crowd of men, women and children being driven along, among them a number of our own. Then I met Mrs. Ehmann, Miss Petersen and Sister Verina. I told them they had told me that we could do nothing till the Mudir came. Just then I saw him go riding by as fast as he could. Mrs. Ehmann said, "Oh! The Mudir is out riding like hell." And the dear woman didn't mean to be profane either. He simply made her think of hell and devils as these things have made all of us think this summer. Truly it seems that hell has boiled over and the world is full of devils. I started home and met Pompish Yester driven along by the police. She asked me to tell the Consul and to go to her house and tell the children to stay in the house and pray. I met one of our zabits and he told me that the order was to kill the last Armenian. This was a lie in order to frighten me enough to let the girls take refuge with the officers who pretended to want to protect them. One who had been in the hospital and taken a house near called to me and said to send the girls to him and he would keep them. Just then a girl raised a window and told me that three of them were there. They had been out and couldn't get back and went there for refuge. In a few minutes I met another girl and she asked me where to go. I told her to go where the others were and I would try to come and get here after dark. I then went to the police station for Margaret who was there trying to find Levon. I persuaded her to come home as it was dark. They had brought in big crowds, men, women and children. All were screaming and crying. The police who were very pleasant were growing furious. I saw it was no use to try to see the Mudir as he probably would be angry to see me there in the confusion and refuse everything. I have never seen the people in such a panic on the street. I could hear crying in every Christian house. Just as the guards were being placed at the gates two of our men started out with a dead body on the stretcher to bury. A boy ran after them, telling them they could not get back. They left the body on the stretcher and ran up to Harpoot. All was quiet there and Herbert knew nothing of what was going on till they came and told him. He left in the beginning of a business meeting and brought the children home leaving Karekin up there. He got here just at dark. Poor children were all upset. Henry could not enjoy his birthday cake. After supper Margaret and I went to the hospital and asked one of our officer patients to help us get the girls home. He was a captain. He told the guard at the gate to let them come and he would be responsible as they were the nurses. We went and found half a dozen of our officer ex-patients there, evidently thinking they were going to have the girls in their own hands for one night. We could see they were much put out to have us bring them home.

November 5

Next morning I sent bread down to the prison. A few had been released, among them Pompish Yester. We made a list of our own people. Herbet took it to the Mudir and he granted us all of them. We went first to the men's prison and secured the release of the men. Then to the women. There we met the Germans with another list whom they were trying to get out. Oh the joy that they showed as they were brought out one at a time. On our list was Yexa's mother, an old deaf woman. She could not hear when her name was called, so I told the police I must go in and get her. They said that the women would pull me to pieces if I went in, that they themselves could not go inside, but I went and what a time I had. Poor things pulling at me and begging me to do something for them. Crowded in there, they had had nothing to eat except what we and the Germans sent and that was not enough. Not room to lie down with nothing but the bare ground, but as part of their prison was without roof they had plenty of air. One of the women who begged me to help her was the wife of one of our professors who was killed among the first. I told her I would try for her, then I found she was on the German list. Oh the despair when our lists were finished and those that were left gave up hope. I will never forget their cries and their faces as the police shoved them back and shut the door. Nor never shall I forget the scene, we and the Germans waiting at the prison door trying to pull out a few helpless women and children while fifty feet away stood the mosque all decorated with flags and crowds of the officials coming in for the service to give thanks to God for the opening of the road between Germany and Turkey. While we were standing there a crowd of three or four hundred women and children from the villages were driven by us to another prison from where they were all sent out the next night. Two nights after it was raining cold November rain. As I put the children to bed I thought of all those women and children out on the mountains somewhere without shelter or food. Then the thought came, "Oh I hope they have killed them before this!" Then I was shocked at the thought, but why should I be? It is the only relief. Friends, homes, honor and hope gone. Everything but life and a sure knowledge that it too must go sooner or later.

November 15

Miss Campbell, Mrs. Riggs, Mr. and Mrs. Pierce and children and Mr. and Mrs. Ernest Riggs and children, started to go to America today. They had an awful time to get arabas and it was with much fear and trembling we saw them start out on that dangerous road, but the Consul and the ambassador urge it. They urge it for all of us, but some of us must stay by the few remaining people to give out relief where we can. I feel a great burden falling on our shoulders with Miss Campbell going, but there were two strong reasons why we wanted her to go. First she is a British subject and we don't know what might be the consequence if she should remain. And the second is that she has engaged herself to an Armenian boy a lot younger than herself and we feel that we cannot approve such a marriage even under favourable circumstances as his character is not such as we can approve and under present circumstances we feel she would be placing her life in the greatest danger. Therefore we were glad to get her away before she married him.

November 25

Thanksgiving. We have it here this year. I knew that folks would not stay till after dark so we had service at 11.30 and dinner at one. Seventeen at table included two Danes and little Bessie, an Armenian, and an American woman and her little boy who is stranded here sick. Her husband, an Armenian, was killed. All of us amidst the hard things we have are truly thankful to be alive. The service was sweet. The dinner was: Barley soup, rice pilav, baked nuts, potatoes mashed, canned corn, turkey and stuffing, pickles, plum jelly, vegetable salad, squash pie, pumpkin pie, tulum cheese, apples, grapes, pears and coffee.

After dinner was the usual weighings; Herbet 178, I 120, Henry 84, Alice 50, Harriet 40. All went home before dark.

November 26

A letter from Grandma, the first for two months. I have nine children in my school now.

December 9

Another "Sevkiat" has just passed through, about six hundred, all young men. I do not know where they came from. The last who passed through were all killed, so the returning zaptias say. I have heard at last something of the Bennyans. They and Mariam Tashjian and Badaskan Varj. hired a man and his donkey to go with them, a Turk of course. He was to take them for eleven liras. He came back and said he took them as far as "Furunjuk" two hours the other side of Malatia and there he was told he must leave them and come back. He did so. We know what this means. Furunjuk is probably one of the biggest slaughter houses in Turkey. I have seen the place years ago. It is a deep gorge running across the Malatia plain. I hope I shall never again see it. It seems it must be filled to the brim with bodies. News comes of Dr. Thom's death in Sivas. Probably from typhus. Last week the Consul came here to find out about some people who had been inquired about from America. Several people were called and questioned, one was Markareed from Huiloo. She came here with many cuts in her back but is well now and is helping with the nursing till time for her confinement. He asked her about a certain family. She said yes they were relatives of hers, and had all been sent and had been killed. He asked her how she knew. She saw them killed. She was with them and was left for dead and when night came she ran away. She thinks she was some days getting here during which time she had nothing but water. She told how the killing was done and where, at Kurdemlik just this side of the lake about five hours from here, and was done with stones and knives.

December 12

Miss McLaren and Miss Shane arrived here from Bitlis. Herbert, Miss Harley and Miss Jacobsen went out to meet them. Their team gave out at Vartateel and Herbert gave one of them his horse and Mahmut gave his to the other. Then Herbert sent Belle and Marie home by the short cut and he walked and brought them here for the night. Miss Petersen, Henry and I went out to meet them but they were so late we had to come home ahead of them.

December 13

Mr. Riggs came down and took them to Harpoot. He said Annie had mumps but when he described it, Herbert said it wasn't mumps.

December 16

Herbert went to Harpoot to see Annie. He was troubled about her. That night he complained of a chilly sensation and thought he had a slight fever.

December 17

They sent for Herbert to go and see Annie as she was bad. He didn't feel well but went. He did not return till night, then it was to tell us that Annie was dead. She died at four o'clock. That night he had a slight chill and fever. The next day [December 18] he told me to go to Harpoot and if I saw he was needed to send the horse for him. Otherwise he would not go as he didn't feel well. I came home in the afternoon and found him in bed. That night he had a hard chill and his fever went up to 104.4. Then he knew he was in for something. I did not want to leave him and go to Harpoot the next day [December 19] for the funeral, but he insisted saying it was a shame to leave Harry and Emma alone in their sorrow. So I went. The fog hung thick. Harry read the scripture about Christ blessing the children, also in Revelation about the white robes. A children's service was held in the Varjaran. Then he took her to the garden and laid her away. I stayed for dinner with Emma and Harry and then hurried home. I found Herbert with a high fever. I had a stove put into his room and gave him a sponge bath. He sat upon his bed by the stove for his bath. He felt better after his bath and slept some, but his fever was high.

December 20

His fever was high, about 105, but he seemed strong and had a good appetite. When his fever was highest he seemed least sick and insisted in walking across the floor and sitting up. I sponged him off many times. At night I had Araxie sit up with him and I slept in the room getting up often to look after him.

December 21

Tuesday was like Monday except for slight deafness. High fever, frequent sponging, some pain and ache in the back of head, kidneys and ankles. Mr. Riggs came up to see him. We thought it recurrent fever. Several doctors had come to see him but Dr. Michael and Izzet Bey were asked to come regularly with Ruth. At night I rubbed his head, back and ankles with liniment and he said the pain all left. That night he had no pain at all but a fever above 104 all night and was wide awake. I got up at midnight and sponged him off and at six I gave him a cold pack. Miss McLaren came and I turned over the hospital and children to her. The cold pack seemed to relieve him and lower his fever but it also weakened him. About 11 o'clock the doctors came, examined and found typhus spots. His fever began rising again and I gave him another cold pack which reduced it but also weakened him. In the afternoon Henry came in and he said, "Henry, if I die will you take care of mother?" Henry began to cry and promised. A little later he said to me, "I am going to die on Sunday." I asked him how he knew and he said he had measured his strength and he thought he had that much but no more. I noticed a decided loss of strength and difficulty in speaking. I tried to dissuade him from his thought of dying, knowing that the thought would react on his strength, but he said "God knows my soul better than you do." He said his work was finished, he had said that many times before. He had felt that God had sent him here just for the work he had done this summer. And oh! He has been a tower of strength. He had been without fear although he knew he might lose his life in his effort to save others. He felt that God sent him back to Turkey just for this. He asked me to call the "girlies" and let them kiss him goodbye. He said "Girlies, I am going to be with Jesus, and Leonard and Annie, won't that be nice?" Harriet answered "Yes." Then I sponged his forehead with alcohol and they kissed him. He asked me to let them come in every day. A little later he asked for the Consul. I sent for him. He came a little after five. Herbert sent me out. A little later I heard him coughing. He seemed to speak with much difficulty. He told me that the Consul had promised to help me in every way possible. He then told the Consul that he could not see what was best for me, but if we should go to America he thought I had better take a house in Oberlin and put the children in school. The consul then left, and he told me he had a message of love to send home, but to wait till he could think just what he wanted to say. He never gave me his message. He then had me rub the back of his head, across his kidneys and his ankles with liniment to take away the pain which had come back. He said, "Now I will seem better and the doctors will be deceived but you and I will understand that it is only the influence of the medicine." A little later he said, "I will be conscious to the end, but I don't think I will sleep any more." A little later I began reading to him from the Bible. He said, "Read about Heaven." I did and he said, "Isn't that beautiful." Then I said, "Doesn't Jesus seem near?" He smiled and said, "Yes." A little later he said, "Possibly I am mistaken, if I stay it will be just for you. You do your best and I'll try." A little later he took his medicine and drank a glass of milk, said he was perfectly comfortable and went to sleep. When he awoke he could not speak, yet he was perfectly conscious. Nor could he take anything on his stomach, and from that time on he took only a few drops of water or lemonade. He made me understand yes or no by closing his eyes or lifting his eyebrows. After three or four hours he could say yes or no in a whisper. He slept and woke all night. He sweated and his fever dropped some. His pulse was weak but regular.

December 23

In the morning, Thursday, fever rose again but on account of his heart they did not allow another cold pack and only a little sponging. I tried him with everything in the morning but could not swallow nothing. He seemed to try but could not. At noon Marie came to help me as I had had but little sleep all the week. I lay down and slept a little. When I got up I could see he was weaker and his fever higher. He could still whisper a few words to me. The doctors injected salt solution hypodermically to supply the need of water, but on account of the condition of the bowels they could not give food enema. The next day they gave it. In the night I wrote to mother and he by a sign sent love. I asked him many times if he had pain but he always said no and once he whispered, "Perfectly comfortable."

December 24

In the morning I brought the children in and he smiled and blew a kiss to them. I then left him for some sleep. They irrigated his bowels and gave food by enema. They said he kept smiling all day and when Henry came in he would follow him with his eyes and smile, but his fever was very high, always above 104 and sometimes above 105. At four o'clock I came back to him. He smiled when he saw me, took my hand, pulled me down, patted my cheek, ran his fingers through my short hair, then with the forefinger of the other hand he pointed upward. I knew he was trying to tell me he was going. I brought in the children. He looked at them and then I sponged off his forehead with alcohol and we all kissed him. After that he did not seem to notice much more. At six I took his temperature. It was 106.6. His heart could only be counted with the stethoscope but it was regular. The doctor said he was becoming unconscious, but for a long time after he would respond to my hand pressure. The doctors wanted to put him into a tepid bath to reduce his fever. I felt that it was of no use but said nothing. We prepared the bath but just as they were ready I saw that he was going. I asked them to examine his heart. Both Dr. Michael and Dr. Izzet Beg examined it and said it would not do to disturb him. His temperature remained at that height to the end. I sent for Miss McLaren and Marie. A cold towel was folded over his head. His head turned slightly to one side, a two weeks' growth of beard was on his face. His quiet eyes turned upward and his lips were parted. I am sure it was not imagination, for several noticed it separately, gradually there stole into his face the likeness of our dying Lord. I noticed it and spoke of it. Henry said, "Mother I noticed it some time ago." Others also had noticed it. There seemed to be a quiet holiness in the room. At last the doctor could no longer hear the heart even with the stethoscope. No trace of pain, no struggle. Oh! To so live that in death we can take on His likeness. "Oh death, where is thy sting?" Henry said, "Oh Mother if I can only be good like that." At 2:25 on Christmas the breath stopped. His soul was gone to be with God. The children were brought in. Harriet thought him asleep. The next morning when we went in to see him the Christlikeness had passed, and there he lay looking as if he were playing sleep as he sometimes did with the girlies ready to jump and laugh and scare them, as we so often did when he tried to steal up and kiss him. He looked so lifelike just as I have seen him look a thousand times when he had obtained something he wanted. All day people were coming and going to take a last look and to speak to me. Emma and Harry came and stayed all day and night. Moslems and Christians were alike in words of sympathy and love. I didn't know people loved him so much. Our own carpenter made the casket of pine boards and stained and varnished it.

December 26

Sunday morning at 9:30 the casket was brought into the dinning room and the folding doors opened and a short service was held in English for our circle and the Germans. Mr. Ehmann read Ps.126. Rom. 8;35-39. Phil. 3;20, 21. Rev. 12; 10, 11. Rev. 14; 13. Rev. 22: 1-5. After this Harry prayed a prayer which seemed to lift us up before the throne of God. Then the body was taken to the hospital where Badv. Vartan held a service in Armenian and afterwards Harry in Turkish. Harry spoke from 1 Cor. 15. The Armenian hymns was "Rise my soul stretch forth thy wings." The Turkish was "The Home of Soul." In the house we had sung "Asleep in Jesus." Then Izzet Beg the Turkish doctor read a paper. Armenian and Turkish young men together bore the casket up that long mountain to the grave. They were accompanied by a company of militia and a squad of police. Also many of the highest officials including the commandant. Also the Armenians. The sun

Dr. Herbert Atkinson (front row with walking stick) with Turkish government and military officials during the war. Dr. Atkinson worked with the Red Cross and took care of soldiers who were wounded at the Russian front.

came out gloriously warm the first few weeks. We laid the precious remain beside our darling baby to await the resurrection morn. It is the first time in Harpoot that the Moslems and Christians have wept together beside an open grave. They sang "The City Foresquare." We stopped with Harry and Emma for dinner and afterward Harry brought us home to begin life alone.

December 27

Many callers have come both Moslems and Christians. All seem to have loved my dear one. Harry came and helped me to receive them. I thank my God always for his presence with me. I am so glad to have Miss McLaren here.

1916

January 1

Another year beginning. Oh God what of pain and trial is before us? "My grace is sufficient for thee." We are invited to Harpoot. I am glad to escape New Year's calls. I took Harriet on my lap and rode Elmas and Miss McLaren rode Albus. Alice and Henry rode the donkey. Miss Petersen also went. We had dinner with Emma and Harry and after dinner we went in to Belle's room where we had a tiny Christmas tree with a few presents for the children and some cocoa. Ruth was sick with what seems to be typhus. We came home in the evening.

January 3

School begins again and I am trying to get a hold of the thread ends of things, but oh! Life seems hard without Herbert!

January 31

One month of the new year has gone. The last two weeks have been hard. One officer who has been in the hospital a long time wants a girl whom I have in the house. Her mother begs me to keep her and she begs to be kept from him. We have kept her for a long time to protect her. At last he turned on me. He wrote a paper two feet long of evils against me and showed it to the commandant and Ser Tabib. At first they were inclined to believe. I did nothing but pray and God turned their hearts. They saw it was all lies, and so sent him out of the hospital and assured me that he should trouble me no more. But there is an attempt on the part of several to bully me and I think to gain control of the hospital. I mean to do my best as long as I can.

February 20

The Russians are said to be drawing near and many Moslems are fleeing. It is said Erzroum has fallen. The remnant of Armenians who are here are trembling for their lives. They fear the Turks will make an end of them before the Russians come. I have just bought material to make a large Red Cross flag. Herbert had two flag staffs put up. If the time comes I will put up the American and the Red Cross flag. I have told our men that if worse comes to worst each one must find a hole in the mountains, but I must not know where it is. I will keep bread in a place where they can find it in the night. Paper money is depreciating in value and we are finding it hard to finance the hospital. Nejib Bey the Ser Tabib is showing an ugly disposition to bully over me and since I have to take Herbert's place in managing the hospital I realise how hard it is and how easy it was for him to be willing to die and leave it all. If it were not for the children how gladly I would join him.

March 20

Kurds in the Dersim are in rebellion. The government sent three regiments of soldiers. Two of them were wiped out. Many of the Turks are fleeing.

March 25

It was a glorious day. Henry and I went to the garden and fixed up our graves. We took Alice and Harriet up to Harpoot and left them there to play.

March 26

Grandma's birthday. A year ago Harriet was burned. We made chocolate cake and all of us wrote to Grandma.

April 2

Nejib Bey is again on the rampage. He demands that we feed the men rice every day. As it would require four dollars a day at the present price of rice we cannot afford it with the amount of Red Cross money we have. He sent word to me if I didn't do it he would close the hospital. I sent word back to close it if he wanted to. I wasn't anxious to do Red Cross work for him, when they were so ungrateful for what we are doing. I also said that within another year his soldiers would be thankful for dry bread. The Chaoush was afraid to carry him my message, so he didn't receive it, but yesterday Mr. Riggs went to see the Commandant on the subject. He is a more sensible man and talked very reasonably. We've heard nothing more. But with only bank notes to buy with, our problem grows daily more serious.

April 4

Pertag was burned today by the Kurds. The line of fighting is drawing nearer. Will it come here and if it does what will it mean to us and our work? Finis? Perhaps so.

April 9

Yesterday two Armenian doctors came here from Constantinople. When they reached Malatia they were told that they would be killed here if they did not change their names and religion. They said they didn't want to die. One said he had a family who were dependent on him and he could not die so he changed. "He that loveth his life more than me is not worthy of me." How our hearts ached for them. Yet this is the story of many. Although this terrible massacre of Armenians has not been for their religion. It has been for political reasons, yet the fact remains that many of those who remained after the first terrible two months have changed their religion in order to be saved, but as we have often seen, it has failed to save them.

April 13

Prayer meeting was here. Mr. Riggs received a letter from Mr. Peet saying that Red Cross funds are cut off all over Turkey. We decided to tell the Commandant on Saturday and offer them a hundred beds in our hospital. They to furnish food and we service.

April 15

We went to the Commandant and told him our funds are cut off and offered him the use of a hundred beds, we to supply labor and all that we can while they supply the rest. They took it very nicely and Nejib Bey came up to make necessary arrangements.

April 17

The change in hospital took place today without special friction. I had called all the hospital staff and prepared them for the change. The Consul has received a telegram from the Ambassador saying that local officials must be specially kind to Americans.

May 9

Enver Pasha, the Minister of War, leaves Sivas today in automobiles for here. He is expected tomorrow night. The Commandant called here. I asked him to invite the gentleman here for tea, if he should come to the hospital. We are putting up the American flag, also the Turkish on the two flagpoles which Herbert had erected. The Red Crescent was strung between the two. How I had wanted the Red Cross, but it was a month too late for that. Great preparations were made everywhere. I put a little American flag on the front porch of our own house. Our thoughts were not altogether as loyal as they might have been. When he rose up eight years ago and deposed Abdul Hamid and brought about the revolution, he was the nation's hero and his welcome would have been whole hearted. But he has now dragged us into this awful war and worst of all he has caused the killing of the

Armenians, not because of their religion, as Abdul Hamid would have done, but because he thought them traitors. Still we must show him honor as he is without doubt the nation's most powerful man.

May 11

Enver Pasha arrived about noon today. He went first to the Vali's house where Miss Petersen and the German sisters helped with the entertainment for him. In the evening his automobile whizzed by and went up to the new hospital. We thought we were left out. Mr. Riggs came down to help receive him if he came, and when he left there we saw he was turning in here. Miss McLaren and I stood on the front porch of the hospital to welcome him while Mr. Riggs went down to the automobile. He said that if I would excuse him he would see the soldiers first and afterward come here, so Miss McLaren and I came home and Mr. Riggs went with him through the wards. He spoke very appreciatingly of Herbert's work to Mr. Riggs. When he came in here he at once asked if I spoke Turkish. On learning that I did he spoke of Herbert and his work and said that to show honor to his memory he wanted to decorate his son with a silver war medal. He asked Henry's age. I went to call Henry. When he came in the great man arose, put his arms around Henry, kissed him, took the medal from his own breast and pinned it on Henry, telling him that that was to show the country's appreciation of Henry's father. Of course we all felt very happy to have the memory of our dear one so honored. He pulled Harriet to him, spoke to her in English and patted Alice on the cheek. The children were charmed with him. We served tea and then he went. That night Henry said, "Oh Mother! What a pity such a nice man should not be a Christian." "Let's pray for him to become a Christian." We have learned that the Commandant told him how Herbert had been doing Red Cross work and had cared for a hundred soldiers for a year under the Red Cross and had at last taken typhus and died. He asked if anything had been done to show him honor. Then he asked if he had children. Then he said, "We will decorate his son in honor of his memory." The medal is a silver star and crescent with the Sultan's insignia and the date [Arabic] (1332) which is the Turkish date.

May 15

Mr. Riggs came down and had Henry put on the medal and go down to call on the commandant to thank him for it.

May 23

Yesterday a large crowd of Kurdish women and children were brought in from the Dersim. More than two thousand I think. They were captured and brought in because the Kurds are in rebellion. It is supposed they are to be sent and killed just as the Armenians were. They were put in the graveyard where the Armenians were kept last summer. This afternoon they were sent back on the Dersim road. Our men said they were taking them out to kill them, while others said a pardon had come for them and they were sending them back to the Dersim.

Badveli Durtad's daughter has come home. She was in Palu teaching at the time of the Sevkiat. She was taken by a Turkish family for a wife to their son. She lived with him as his wife and he wanted to marry her but she constantly refused. When the Kurds burned Palu they came to Aguntseek as refugees. She wrote to her mother that she could not tell how hungry she was nor how sore her feet were. At last she persuaded her so-called husband to bring her for a fifteen day visit to her parents. He brought her. He was a nice appearing young fellow, but of course he is a Moslem. She seemed to like him and he her. He never had tried to change her religion. When he came to take her, her parents would not let her go. He was very much hurt about it, but they managed to scare him away and she stayed at home.

May 24

I have just learned that the hospital cook, Nevart, has been carrying on an affair with the Chaoush. There was nothing to do but dismiss her as the proof was very evident. This made the Chaoush angry and he gave a list of the Armenian workers who are here to the police mudir and told him they were "furars" who were hiding here. A police came up for them yesterday and I knew at once what was the reason of it all. We refused to deliver over the boys and Miss McLaren and I went straight to the Commandant and found that he knew nothing about it. At last he found out, then he told us to send them all down and let them be written and then bring them back. We found the police had gone when we returned and so we took them ourselves. In the evening Chaoush came to me and declared he had no connection with Nevart. He also denied having given in the names.

May 26

Herbert's birthday. A full day of sweet memories of the one who is gone. I had intended making a cake for I cannot let the children pass over this day without remembering it. We had our first green peas. Miss Harley and Miss Shane sent word they were coming to supper. So I also invited Marie and Miss Petersen. I set the table as nicely as I could, put a bunch of carnations on it with Herbert's picture. We had peas, hot scones and butter, and the cake which was delicious and cocoa.

May 30

Yesterday the Governor sent up for our boys and took them. I went to the Commandant. He said they were soldiers and if the doctors said they were needed they would send them back. We went to Ourfan Bey and he said that we didn't need all but that they would give us four, put four in the Merkez hospital and four in the Inshaat. He sent us home to make out a list of those we preferred. When we sent the list they said that we didn't need any of them but they were all to be sent to Malatia to work on the roads. This morning word comes that some of them escaped during the night and one broke his leg. He is hidden in a house now and sends word to us. I don't know what I can do.

June 4

The boys have all escaped but four. Three were given back to us and one was sent away. The police came here and searched for them.

June 7

Harriet's fifth birthday. She had a very happy day. She received some dolls and a doll cradle. In the afternoon she had a party with the little Ehmann children and several little Armenian friends. Harriet said "Mother is there another man anywhere just like Father?" I said, "No." Then she said, "Who can I marry when I get big?"

July 3

This is my 46th birthday. I was wakened by my dear boy Henry kissing me and wishing me a happy birthday and then came Alice. The two were up, and downstairs early. Then Harriet and I got up and Harriet kissed me forty-six times. What would I do without these dear children. At breakfast I found on my plate their little birthday gifts and a dear note from Henry. I was told after prayers that I was not to go to the kitchen all day and not to go anywhere without permission. I knew that Henry boy was baking a birthday cake. So I was deaf and blind all day. I rested and read. I was told that I must "dress for supper." At six o'clock the door suddenly opened and in came all the Harpoot station. Then the dinning room was opened and there was the table all decorated in red, white and blue and places for twelve. A delicious chicken stew was served with new potatoes and bread and butter. Afterwards the birthday cake and ice cream. The latter was indeed a surprise. And those dear children and Auntie Kate had planned that all and not even Harriet had peeped to me, though when we were waiting for desert if she couldn't have whispered to Aunt Emma and told her that ice cream was coming, she would have had to tell me as she could not have held in. As we were going to bed Henry told me of how he had worked and schemed to do everything without my knowing.

July 4

We put a little flag out on the front porch this morning in honor of the day and at 10:30 we all went to the consulate to call. That was our Fourth

July 20

I have been to call on Digin Vergene this morning. Her husband was a man of some wealth. Twenty five years ago he went to America and became a citizen, then he went to Liverpool ten years ago and married this girl from Adana. He retained his American citizenship but just before the war he with his wife and children returned here, and he took again his Turkish citizenship in order to regain some property here. Then the war came on and he lost his right of American protection. Last July he was sent in the "Sevkiat" with his wife and children. He was delivered into the hands of a powerful Kurd whose men were sent to do the killing. This man was taken from the araba and killed before the eyes of his wife and children. The Kurd saw the wife who is a pretty woman. He took her to his home and wanted to marry her, but his own wife made such a fuss that he soon decided not to marry her. She also refused to marry him, but she was in his power and was not allowed to go out. She soon became pregnant. In May he offended the Vali and was put in prison. Then her baby was born, she begs him to let her go as she will not marry him, but he refuses, says he loves her. When her baby was born he sent her money from the prison but it never reached her. She was almost starving. Now his brother has come and given her money for food. She wants to run away as he comes out of prison in ten days. She seems a beautiful Christian. She has her English Bible and hymn book. She has well to do relatives in America who would help her if they knew. Her body has suffered every shame but her soul is untouched.

July 20

Henry and Uncle Harry went to the Ice Cave and say they went to the bottom.

August 10

My little family will all be with me again. Alice and Harriet have been at the garden two weeks, the longest they have ever been away. Harriet came home this morning and Alice and Aunt Kate come tonight. Harriet has just been telling me a little story. Last night looking at the stars she saw an eye. It was Father's looking right at her, then she saw another and it was Annie, then another which she did not know at first, then she saw it was Leonard. Then she saw another, and whom do you suppose it was? It was Jesus, and they were all looking right down at them while they were listening to the gramophone at the garden.

September 7

They have all been begging me to go to the garden for a rest, as I have not been well. Miss McLaren tried to go on August 16 for Miss Shane's birthday. She took Harriet on the horse with her and Alice and Henry were on the donkey. She saw her saddle was slipping backward and got off to fix it. It turned and she fell and sprained her knee. She came home leaving the children upon the hillside promising that Osman should go back with them. Mr. Riggs came on and took the two little girls. Henry and Osman went exploring and found a blackberry patch, gathered some berries and went on to the party. When they wanted me to go Marie came to take my place. I took Henry and went, but had a sick headache so did not enjoy my ride. It was awfully cold there. I stayed my week which seemed awfully long.

September 14

I started to come home from the garden. Henry came the short way and I came the Perteg road. My horse fell on a bad place on the mountain and I sprained my thumb. It was a bad sprain as both thumb joints were sprained.

October 13

Friday night Hovsep came in terribly excited with Mehmet and told me that he was out walking around the walls and the nefers came out and caught him saying he was running away to the Dersim. Mehmet then told me that several of the boys were running away and they caught them and they had their chantas on their backs. I believed Mehmet and sent for all the nefers and all the Armenians. They all came but Suren the head wound dresser. When I asked for him they said he had gone. Then I knew they were all trying to go. The nefers gave notice at the Merkez for these boys were soldiers and of course they had run away to the Russians. The Merkez Mudir told Osman to tie them and bring them to the Merkez or else lock them in a room here. Osman did not do it but watched the hospital all night. Next morning they both escaped. Nazaret came into our kitchen, then our cook went out over to the hospital and engaged the guard in conversation and he slipped out at the side gate. As soon as I was up word was brought to me that he had gone. A little later Merkez Mudir came and demanded him of me. I said that he was gone and I did not know where he was. Then he said he was last seen entering our kitchen and he thought he was hidden in our house. I said he was perfectly welcome to search, that if he was here I did not know it. I felt sure he was not here. I took the keys, opened every place and he looked. Henry amused us all by getting down and looking under the stove. Then he went to the hospital and in a minute I followed him. The patients and nefers were all in the hall and also a large crowd of clinic patients who had come for the doctor. And in the middle of the hall this Mudir had met Osman and was beating him with his stick because he had let the boys escape. As soon as I stepped into the hall I called him to stop it, and when he did not, I ran up and caught him by the shoulder and told him to stop it and he stopped looking at me in surprise. But he sent Osman to the Merkez and put him in prison. I had no one to do my marketing so I waited an hour or two and then went down and explained that Osman had my money and accounts and asked permission to see him. This they allowed and even let him come with me to the market under guard and do my buying. Osman wanted me to ask for his release but I told him it was better to wait a little. That afternoon the Mudir sent his salaams to me and asked if I would give him a bedstead and the one who gave the message said it would be well for me to give it and then he would give Osman back. This made me awfully angry and I said "No" I would not give a bribe and I told the messenger what I thought of such an order. Then I sent my salaams to him and told him our bedsteads were all occupied by sick soldiers. I think the messenger probably told him how angry I was and he probably remembered that he had taken Osman away from me once before and I had gone to the Commandant and got him back in a hurry. He didn't want me to go again. So that night he called Osman and asked him why he didn't obey his orders and lock up those boys. Osman apologised but the Mudir said, "You were afraid of Madam, you know you were weren't you?" Osman admitted that he was. When Osman told me about it I said, "Why Osman, were you afraid of me?" He said "Yes, Hanum, what would you have said if I had done that?" The Mudir sent him back that night.

October 28

Today we were shocked at the hanging of thirteen Armenian prisoners in the market place. One of them was Muggerditch, the servant of Dr. Smith and a boy whom we all loved. He has been in prison a year and a half. We have tried hard to save him but we were shocked when we heard they had been hanged.

Another one of our boys has run away to Dersim.

November 1

The German military doctor, Liebert came here to do his operating.

November 30

Thanksgiving was at the Riggs'. We all went up except Miss McLaren who is not able to walk yet. There is a great deal of discontent with Dr. Liebert

December 4

I had a talk with Dr. Liebert which was very satisfactory to me and hereafter we will understand each other better.

December 8

I heard that Dr. Liebert was to be removed. I went and had a talk with the Ser Tabib after which he consented to leave him here. The feeling against him is very strong.

December 16

I was taken with a bad dysentery. Dr. Liebert was sick at the same time but Dr. Nickau came and took care of me till Dr. Liebert was again well.

December 25

Dear Herbert has been a year in Heaven. I had Christmas here as I felt it would be easier here in our own home than anywhere else. We had a simple little tree and the children were happy with their dollies. Not many presents except to the children.

December 26

I had Christmas for the soldiers. Schmitter helped me. Henry ran the gramophone. Each one received a pear and a picture card. I sang and read the story of Christ and talked about God's love. All were very happy

December 27

I had Christmas for the Armenians. I gave each one a card, a pear and some little present. They were all happy

1917

January 1

Another New Year. What will it bring to us? A few callers but nothing compared with the past.

January 14

Alice is sick with appendicitis.

January 21

Dr. Liebert and Dr. Nickau took dinner with us today. Alice is better.

January 22

Alice, worse again, is back in bed.

February 7

The four German doctors, Mr. and Mrs. Ehmann and I were invited to the Riggs' for dinner. It was a lovely day and I rode up on horseback with the doctors. In the evening news came of the withdrawal of the ambassador from Berlin.

February 12

We all went to see the three doctors start. I am sorry to lose Dr. Liebert.

February 19

Dr. Sophocles has been sent to work with me here. He is a very good surgeon.

March 26

We celebrated Grandma's birthday today quietly. I baked a sponge cake and Miss Petersen came to help us eat it.

April 9

This morning Mardiros was called home and his house searched. I went with him. They took him to prison and I locked up the pharmacy. I went to the Commandant and asked the reason which he did not tell me; but I learned from other sources that he was thought to have been sending people to the Dersim, but I knew he was not guilty. The next day Pompish, the woman who assists in relief work was taken. Miss McLaren and I went to the police station with her. She was pregnant and her time was at hand. Pains began and we feared that her time would come right there. At last she was sent to prison and after a time her pain stopped.

April 11

Iskender Bey, the staff doctor, called here. He speaks English as well as I do. I told him my trouble and he advised me to tell it all to Ibrahim Tali Bey, the head army doctor. I did so and he promised to do his best to see that no injustice was done.

April 14

Mardiros was released from prison.

April 16

Pompish Yghaper was released.

April 28

News came that diplomatic relations have been broken with America and the US flag came down. We do not know what the next step will be. Mrs. Riggs is down sick with typhus, this is her sixth day.

April 27

Emma passed away today and we have all decided to go.

Mrs. Atkinson after her return to the United States.

Appendix

[The following 1917 report, "Statement on Armenian Atrocities in Harpoot Region," by Mrs. Tacy W. Atkinson, was submitted to James L. Barton, for an American official inquiry regarding the treatment of Christians in the Ottoman Empire during World War I.]*

The following account of the events in Turkey during the past three years as I have see them, and as they have had an effect upon our work in the Annie Tracy Riggs Hospital. This report is not intended as a publication, but should any part or parts of it be published, names and places are requested to be concealed.

In August, 1914, Dr. Atkinson was called before the Turkish authorities and told that the Annie Tacy Riggs Hospital was to be requisitioned for the use of the soldiers. He answered that they had no right and could not do this without his consent and that of the American Consul; but he told them that he would be glad to help them in their time of need by taking a number of their sick into the hospital and caring for them, but that the government should provide for their expense as we had no means for that. They accepted his offer and in September we prepared twenty beds in the lower wards for their use. They sent patients, also some private soldiers to help care for them. A little later we gave them 60 and still later 100 beds. The patients were Turks, Kurds and Armenians. They were all very thankful to us for what we did for them. They came in late one night and Miss Campbell and I were up till ten o'clock bathing them and getting them to bed. We heard many such remarks as "You mustn't put your shoes or your bread in your bed. Things are clean here." There seemed to be no difference in the government's treatment of Christian and Moslem soldiers. Some of each were sent to us both as patients and as servants.

---

*. This is the account Tacy Atkinson wrote in 1917, following her return to the United States, when she was asked to write a report on the destruction of Armenians in Kharpert. She wrote her account without the benefit of her diaries, which were hidden away in central Turkey. Her statement can be found at Houghton Library, Cambridge, Mass., document ABC16.9.7/25B/156A. An abridged copy of this report was included in a series of American missionary reports which were sent to the United States government in 1918 regarding the destruction of Christian communities in Ottoman Turkey. See James L. Barton, *"Turkish Atrocities" The Treatment of Christian Communities in the Ottoman Empire, 1915-17,* Ara Sarafian, ed. (Ann Arbor: Gomidas Institute, 1998). Another abridged copy of Atkinson's report appeared in the Armenian Review, 1976. The present publication is the full text by Tacy Atkinson, which has been silently edited for spelling errors and basic formatting.

We told the authorities that it was our custom to have prayers every day and special services on Sundays. They made no objection and we began giving them the Gospel straight and we found them deeply interested. One Sunday I went with Dr. Atkinson to a village, the service being left in the hands of Pastor Vartan, one of our most earnest workers. When we returned at night those men all began talking at once trying to tell us something. At first we could not understand nothing, then we learned that they were trying to tell of the sermon which gave them the simple plan of salvation. I do not know how much of it they really grasped, but their eagerness to tell it was a rebuke to me.

I spent many precious hours with those men trying to teach them the love of God, for there is nothing of love in their religion, and I think the human heart is much the same, all responding to love. One man said, "I can now understand why you Americans are so much more merciful than we. You learn it from your religion." They often said, "Why do you do all these things for us? Why do you love us so much?" Our answer was that we loved God and He loved the whole world, and sent Jesus to teach us that love and we must love others and teach it to them.

After a time our evening prayers began to be attended by other men in the barracks. These came because they were deeply interested. I felt that a number of them began to love Jesus in their hearts.

One teacher, whose hand had been amputated interested me much but the way did not open for a personal conversation for a long time. One day he called me to him and began to read from 1st John. He read on and on, exclaiming "how beautiful!" He went out of the hospital the next day, but I felt that the seed had been sown. They all seemed glad to learn our hymns and sang them with energy. I tried to teach them hymns that would tell the story of Christ.

In February we were told that we must stop the formality of the service, as complaint might be made to Constantinople and that would bring trouble on the authorities there. The officer who told me said, "Talk and sing and pray all you like, but stop the formality."

In June, when the Armenian troubles began we thought best to separate the Armenians from the Moslems in the services, for our services still went on with but little change, only dropping a little of the formality. I took the Moslems and Pastor Vartan took the Armenians. Even when the terrible things were happening all around us I still felt that the power of the Gospel gripped the hearts of these men, even though some of them had been engaged in the terrible work. Mutassarif, or head man from Moush, came to us to die after having done the most dreadful work in Moush. I sang to him one day, and talked with him. He said, "Oh, I have never heard such words before in my life." I thought that perhaps if he had heard such words before he might not have done the awful deeds he had done. If we want to stop the atrocities in Turkey wouldn't it be the surest way to open the political door so that the Gospel of love might be given to the men who are doing these things?

In August, 1915, a fanatical officer told the commandant that we were making Christians of Turkish soldiers; that if we did not stop it he would write to Constantinople. The commandant told us that it was our hospital and he could not say we must not do it, but if it continued, he would have to take the soldiers out of the hospital. For a time we stopped all services, but later they gave permission for me to sing and talk, but not to read the Bible and pray. We were not hindered in this until we left.

The first of January, 1915 Red Cross funds came to us for keeping 100 soldiers. We then put in a hundred beds, but the need at that time was so great, as men were dying in the streets from typhus, that we often took in a hundred and thirty or forty. We counted the floor space as our limit, instead of beds or bedding. As we provided food and clothing, we were able to make them more comfortable than they were in other hospitals. Those were hard times. Dr. Atkinson was sick in January with influenza. Miss Jacobsen, the nurse, and I each had typhus and help was short. Doctor tried to do a great deal more than he was able to do. The hospital was always full. Sick soldiers having money often gave bribes to the Turkish officers in order to get into our hospital. Doctor was loved and trusted by all.

In the spring we began to notice that there was a fear among the Armenian soldiers. One Armenian in his delirium kept saying, "Count the Armenians, count the Armenians." And when the nurse was not near him one night he cut his throat with the tin cover of his sputum cup. The schools in Harpoot had been closed and most of the buildings taken for soldiers. Boys too young for soldier duties began coming to us, asking for work and wanting only food in return. What they really wanted was safety, and they thought to be identified with the hospital would be the safest thing for them. Doctor gave work and made work for them when he didn't have it to give. One young man in our employ was put in prison because another young man was found with a letter in his pocket addressed to this Toros of ours, saying that the Russians were near and that soon we should be under the Russian flag. This was considered treason. Doctor Atkinson tried in every way but could not secure his release. He was condemned to be exiled for ten years and the boy who had written the letter to be hung. For the time they were kept in prison. In May a number of the teachers in Euphrates College and professors were arrested without any reason being given so far as I know.

Early in June things being bad in Diarbekir, Dr. Smith sent for help. Mr. Harry Riggs went to his assistance. Not being able to help matters any, Mr. Riggs returned bringing Mrs. Smith with him. Dr. Atkinson was at this time in bed with an attack of erysipelas.

On the morning of June 7th, I heard a violent ringing on the telephone bell. Mr. Pierce was in the city and he had learned that the garden where all the other missionaries were was surrounded by Turkish soldiers, and they were searching for papers. Mrs. Smith was the cause. She had brought copy of a telegraphic code in order to communicate with her husband while she was away from him. They had found this. They found nothing objectionable among the missionaries, but they took the telephone away and for a time the missionaries up there were regarded with suspicion and treated rather badly. After a time this was overcome by the straightforward conduct of the missionaries.

Just at this time some bombs were found by an Armenian. Before this time the Armenians were told to give up their arms and many had done so, but others had not. Then the houses and persons were searched for arms and incriminating papers. Many were imprisoned and tortured to make them confess to having arms. Villages were surrounded, houses were searched and the people beaten. I went one day to one of our near villages to see about some of our friends. It was Sunday, guards were around the city, but they let me pass. Perfect stillness reigned. I went to one house and found the family sitting in a circle on the floor. The father was in prison and an expression of terror was written on every face. The garden had been dug two or three feet deep in the search for arms. I went to another house. The wife was alone with her little ones. Her husband, the Pastor of the village, had taken refuge with us in the hospital. I told her that I knew his whereabouts and that he was well, but did not tell her where he was, in order that she might not know if questioned. In returning I saw a crowd of police in a side street. I asked an old woman what it meant. She said they were searching the house. All was perfectly quiet, but I was followed everywhere by ugly looks from the Moslems, both civil and military. One soldier scowled after me in an exceptionally rude manner, evidently trying to frighten me by his looks. I didn't want him to think me afraid of him, and besides I had learned that to take one of them by surprise I had him on the run. So I suddenly turned on him, smiled and asked him if he had not been in our hospital sick the winter before. He stammered, looked confused, and said, "Yes," which was false, for I had never seen him before. I told him I hoped he was well. He smiled, thanked me and made his deepest bow, and I went on leaving him staring, but with a different expression on his face.

At this time we tried to make friends with every police with whom we came in contact and we found that such friendships were a great help to us.

Every day reports came from Harpoot, three miles away, of the terrible torturing of prisoners. One day a boy came to us coming around a distance of five hours, fifteen miles, in order not to be searched. In the hem of his garment he had a little cigarette paper. It was asking for poison for three of our College professors and one merchant, saying they could no longer stand the torturing and they wanted to die. In Mezereh there was no torturing in prisons, but as Harpoot was under the government of a very wicked man things were much worse there.

About this time the Armenian soldiers were called in from the army and shut in a large building near us called the Red Konak. They were kept there a day or two without food or drink. When people came bringing food or water they were driven away. These men were all sent away one night. The officers said they were sent to Aleppo to work on the roads, but rumors started from Turkish sources were that they had all been killed. We never heard of them again. At this time torturing, searching and beating were going on in nearly all the villages, so far as we could hear. But in Mezereh, the seat of government, there was no torturing. Many people began coming to us for refuge and our house and hospital were full. A massacre was expected every day. Crowds of armed Kurds were seen moving about, who a short time before had been released from the prisons. Often policemen came to our door after the men who were thought to be there. It so happened that they never asked for one who was there at the time. They always took our word as truth. Once I called in a policeman and asked him the cause of all the trouble. He asked me if I knew what had been done in Van. He told me that Van had been taken over by revolutionary Armenians and not by Russians. He also told of outrages which had been committed by Armenians on the Turkish people. Whether true or not he, evidently, believed them. The commandant also old Doctor Atkinson and me together that the number of desertions among the Armenians on the Russian frontier and the number of traitors that had been found was the cause of all the trouble. Almost any hour in the day we could see policemen taking Armenian men to prison. Men no longer dared go out anywhere. Near the end of June the prisoners from Harpoot were brought down to Mezereh prison. They consisted of college professors and teachers and the most influential men of the community. They were kept there a day or two and then sent out from the prison at night and for a long time nothing was heard from them. Villagers who saw them pass told us that they were bound together and some who were weak from their tortures were bound between stronger ones and dragged. After some weeks some little boys who belonged to a crowd of villagers had fallen in with these men, were brought back by some Turks who had saved them. They said these men were taken up in the mountains near Bakhur Maden, were shot and the leading ones were afterwards beheaded to make sure that they were dead. It was then announced that the whole population of Armenians were to be deported to Oorfa. They were given five days to make preparations. On July 1, 1915, the first crowd was to be sent from Mezereh. The people began selling and giving away their property and when they did not sell, the police sold for them. One could not help but think of vultures to go down the street and see Turkish men, women and children carrying away household goods for which they had paid nearly nothing. We wanted to store their things for them, but the government forbade it, though they told us we could buy what we wished. They also gave permission for us to keep their money for them. We bought large supplies of food stuffs filling everything. We also took in thousands of liras in gold. This was all saved for them and done with according to their directions. There were many who had no money and nothing to sell. To these we gave money. We also made knapsacks, filling them with bread; at the same time giving all the comfort, advice and courage that we could. Hundreds came begging us to take them or their daughters or their children into the hospital. We did take all we could, but the authorities were constantly sending word to us not to meddle with government matters, or they would have to come and take all the Armenians we had in the hospital.

A small crowd went out on July 1st and a large one was to go July 3rd. On July 2nd, the first crowd arrived from Erzroom. It consisted of women and children from wealthy families, but not a male among them above twelve years. Doctor was busy that afternoon, but Henry and I went with Consul Davis to hear their story. They had been on the road two months, had started out with horses and household goods together with the men of their families. Within a day or two they were attacked by Kurds, probably those who had been released from prison, and all their men and boys killed and many of their girls carried away. They were robbed and stripped of all but one or two garments. Their guards made pretense of defending them, but that it was only a bluff was shown by their killing only two Kurds, while the Kurds killed all the Armenian men and none of the guards. Their guards then stopped at a village and took clothing for them. These rich women were regarded as special prizes and after this first day we were not permitted to see them. They were kept prisoners in a building and so far as we could learn were sought in marriage by the Turks, probably in order to get their property. They seemed to melt away somewhere and after a few weeks the few that were left were allowed to come out and take houses in Mezereh.

Our second crowd started July 3rd. We went early, by five in the morning, among the people and told them what we had learned from the Erzroom women and warned them not to take much money and advised them to dress their boys as girls. Some few boys took this advice and escaped, but Vali had promised them that they were to go in safety and they believed him and went without trouble. Every few days a crowd was sent from Mezereh or the nearby villages. We helped them all we could to get off. Some of those who had taken refuge in the hospital went home and prepared to go. Men were regarded as fortunate who were allowed to go with their families, for all the time arrests were being made and men were thrown into prison. But the prisons were constantly being emptied at night; where these prisoners went we do not yet know.

Dr. Atkinson secured a promise from both the Vali and the Commandant that the hospital workers should not be taken. But about July 10th, as I remember, the military policeman came to take the Armenian soldiers who were working in the hospital to the prison. There were nine of them, but one, Suren, brightest of them, hid in the basement and one of the girls covered him with shavings, but the police had seen him and were angry. They said that if he were not found they would come back with orders to take every Armenian in the hospital, and we knew they would do it. We took the eight into our house for a few minutes of prayer and Doctor told them he would do all in his power to save them. When they had gone he called the girls and told them of the threat of the police and said that we ought not to risk two or three hundred lives for the sake of one. They went and brought out Suren and he was willing to go when he knew what it meant to the rest. Doctor went with him and gave him up to the police. We sent food to the prison each day for our boys as food was not provided for the prisoners, and Doctor turned every stone for their release. While they were there our pharmacist from Harpoot, Melkon Luledjian, was taken. He was thrown into prison with eight hundred business men and the same night they were bound by threes and sent out without food. They were robbed and taken about nine hours' distance into the mountains to the northwest, and there in broad daylight they were taken up into a narrow valley and made to sit down. Then the order was given to fire. Several rounds were fired into them and then the order was given to use the bayonet. At this Melkon broke the ropes that bound him and ran. Several others did the same. They fired after them but did not touch Melkon. He ran on and on, not knowing where he was running. The others ran to a village, told this story to the villagers and were followed by the soldiers and retaken, but Melkon ran on. In the middle of the night he found himself in Mezereh. He came to the hospital, slipped by the night nurse and to Miss Campbell's room. She put him into her inner room; she herself sleeping on the porch, and the next morning told us about it and we knew for the first time just what was happening to the men who were sent out from prison and what would happen to our boys if we could not save them. The villagers also spread the story of those who had escaped and the people woke up to the terrible truth. That night we took Melkon over to our house and hid him for a day or two, but we were afraid he might be found there; so early one morning we dressed him as a Turkish woman and sent him to Harpoot where he was hidden by a Turk for a time.

I found that I could go about the prisons and by passing friendly remarks to the guard could do about as I liked, while Doctor, being a man, must be a little more dignified. So he went to the authorities when formal protests and requests were to be made, while I did the running about and would go to the officers when I wanted to beg for something. They had great respect for him and often did what he asked, but not always. They refused to spare our boys who had been in prison four days. We were expecting every night that they would be sent out. I went to the prison and slipped a handful of safety razor blades to them telling them Melkon's story. I told them that if they were bound and sent that they were to cut their ropes nearly in two but not quite, then when the shooting should begin, they were to break their ropes and run. They were sent that night, but I never knew their fate. After all Doctor's efforts to save them had failed, I, with Doctor's advice, decided to go to the Commandant and beg for them. I went with fear and trembling, for I had never gone to a high official before and I could not forget that I was a woman and he an officer. I went and begged for all of our boys, but for Suren I especially begged, as we had delivered him up and we felt that his blood would be upon us if he were killed. I told the Commandant that we could not bear this. He assured me that they would not be killed, but would be sent to work on the roads. Then I told him of the scene described by Melkon, but did not tell how I knew it. He shrugged his shoulders and said, "If that be true, I have not heard it," but he drew a line under Suren's name and promised to go to the Vali about it. That afternoon Suren was released. He was never touched again. He was always afterward spoken of as the young man who had been given to me. For fifteen months he was a great help to us in the hospital; then he escaped to Russia by way of the Dersim.

At this time thousands were coming to us from the north, Erzroom, Erzingan, Ordou, Trebizond and many other places. In the second company that came there were about eight thousand. They said they were about thirty thousand when they started. They had been attacked seven times by Kurds, robbed and the men killed, but it had been impossible to kill all the men as the company was so large. Some men reached us. They were camped outside Mezereh several days. Their tales were most pitiful. Men killed, girls carried away, women threw themselves and their children into the streams, preferring death by drowning rather than the suffering that they must bear from hunger and abuse. Homes, friends and honor gone, for what should they care to live? How often did we tell them that no man could take away their honor, so long as the heart was pure. Picture eight thousand people, mostly women and children, camped out in the glaring July sun with only the remains of the clothing with which they had left their homes two months before and not half enough food to satisfy their hunger. Sometimes they stretched up a bit of gunny sack or an old apron to protect them from the sun. Their bodies were covered with vermin. Often there were great sores on arms, necks and faces from the burning of the sun. Many were sick with dysentery and malaria. The guards surrounded them so that there was no chance of escape. We found two of our college boys among them, both sick. We asked to be allowed to take them to our hospital, but were refused. The people begged us to help them; often we saw new-born babies that had never even been washed, wrapped in some dirty rag. When we would stop for a moment we would be surrounded, all begging for medicine, or food, but especially that we should help them to escape. We always told them that if they could escape we would take them into the hospital. Must our own people who were being sent away come to this? We have reason now to believe that their suffering was even worse than this. So far as we know, not any man was sent from us went through alive, and I have been told by missionaries that many of our Harpoot women and children reached Aleppo and Oorfa without a single garment. One man, a Turk, whom I hope to meet some day in the kingdom of Heaven, was in charge of the Red Crescent Hospital. He sent away all his sick soldiers and kept a horse and wagon busy all the time going between his hospital and the camp, bringing in the sick. He rented other buildings and filled them all. He had no means sufficient to provide for so many and many died, but he had done what he could. (We were not allowed to do this. He afterwards lost his position.)

Many of these people, especially children, were rescued by the Turks, who took them into their homes. Many died while there, but after a few days they were all sent on somewhere. I think they went only a short distance up into the mountains, for our vilayet seemed to be the slaughterhouse of the empire. In a few days another crowd would come and camp in the same place. This was kept up for two months or more. We went many times and saw them. Their story was always about the same. Our people seeing them began to be afraid to go, and when they were bidden to go they would hide. Turkish people opened their homes and took in great numbers, especially women and children, though they were forbidden by the government to do so.

Nearly all the men had been taken by the middle of July and sent out at night from the prisons. One afternoon Dr. Atkinson was coming down from Harpoot when a crowd of old men and boys had been collected and were being driven down from Harpoot to the Mezereh prison. Wives and daughters followed them out weeping. They were driven back with the butts of the soldiers' guns. Many of the old men had been for years members of our church. When one would totter and fall he was struck with the butt of a gun to bring him to his feet. Doctor came behind them all the way down the mountain. When he reached home his nerves completely went to pieces and he had hard work to pull himself together again, but there was little time in those days to dwell upon one horror, for another was so soon upon us. The poor old men were soon sent out, but not far.

One night we were wakened by shooting. Looking toward Mezereh we saw a fire. Next morning we learned that a part of the prison had burned where the prisoners who were under sentence were kept. Our Toros was among them. Also a doctor who had often assisted Dr. Atkinson. Some of the prisoners, trying to escape, had been shot; the rest were burned in the prison. These two were of the latter. There were two stories given as to the cause of the fire. One was that the prisoners were ordered to be sent out. They refused to go and their officer ordered them to be burned in the prison. This might easily be true as that part of the building was old and not worth much. Another story was that they were ordered out and that a big fat man from Husenik set fire to the bedding. We have some reason for believing the latter story. A few days before we had heard of this very Husenik man that he was trying to get material to make a bomb to blow up the prison in case they were sent. He must have been nearly insane. Toros and the Doctor were his friends. I went to the prison and begged them to use their influence against it. They pointed to a pile of ropes lying in the corner and said that they knew that they were to be bound and sent out. They didn't care much what they did.

One afternoon our hospital was suddenly surrounded by police. Doctor was in the operating room amputating the leg of a Turkish officer. They had come to take the Armenians—all that we had in the hospital. I do not know how many there were, but there must have been two or three hundred. I went to tell Doctor but finding him in the middle of the operation, it didn't seem right to tell him. I went back and told the doctor who had come with the police that they must wait. I seated them on the front porch and sat down with them. I told them how much it hurt us to give up these people who had come to us for refuge. They said that they were sent by the Commandant, who at that time was also acting as Vali and that they must obey orders. I asked them to wait until I could go and see the Commandant and ask him to change the orders. I went, asking God all the way to show me what to say. The Commandant said that he was not doing it, but that it was the work of the Chief of Police acting under the Vali's instructions. Then I asked to see the Chief of Police. He came in and I had the two together, the two whose hands were perhaps the redest of any two men in Turkey. I asked them not to take these people away from us, but to let us have a week to send them out and then they could take them from outside. I begged them to be merciful as they would want God to be merciful with them. I asked them what they were going to answer when they were called up before God. They said they didn't know but if the Osmanli government were going to stand these Armenians must be disposed of. The Commandant told me that if the young man, Suren, whom he had given to me were spared that I should be thankful, as the order was that not one Armenian should remain. He also said that the order was that no man should go outside the vilayet. I believe that order was carried out. They asked me if I would guarantee that our people would not run away provided they allowed them to be sent out of the hospital as I had requested. I told them that this was not my work, that they had police who could see to that. Of course I knew they would run away and I knew that I would help them. Then they thought they would frighten me, so the Commandant said, "If you and your husband continue to meddle in the affairs of the government and we allow you to do it, they will take you and your husband and me and this Chief of Police and they will put us all into prison together." I said, "I am not one bit afraid of prison, nor of anything man can do, nor of death, if it be necessary, but I am afraid of sin, and this is sin." Then he began to walk the floor and say, "What shall we do? What shall we do?" They refused my request and I went home and found Dr. Atkinson out on the front porch with a number of the Armenians. He had gone through the hospital with the Turkish doctor and the police and had taken them straight past one room filled with young men and another filled with women and girls. He had also succeeded in saving several who were in the wards. One of them was our pastor Vartan. Another, one of the college professors who was then with us. The heart of the Chief of Police had been touched by my talk with him and he followed me back to the hospital. As soon as he came he gave orders that the girls should not be taken that day. Then he began to sort out those on the front porch who seemed too weak to go and we began to help him. Some had come out dressed in hospital clothes. We called attention to this and sent them back to change. In confusion they dodged down into the basement and hid in the shavings. He asked some of our Turkish officer patients if there were many more. He also asked if there were none in our house. The house was full, and they knew it, but they said, "No, none." They at last took only twelve men. These, of course, were put in prison and sent out and we never heard of them again, but we were very thankful that the number was so small. That night we found that Henry had filled the shelves in our bedroom closets with boys and he has since told me that he had some down in the cistern and that some crawled through a dry sewer. The Chief of Police has never since refused to give me anything I have ever asked.

One day when we were eating dinner we heard a knock at the door and in walked Professor Luledjian. He had been one of the number who had been in prison and while being tortured had sent to us asking for poison. He told us of how he had been tortured, and how the Kaimakam (Mayor) had come in himself and with his own hands had beaten him. While he was beaten, himself, he could hear the cries of his friends and his own brother as they were being beaten. His fingers even then were torn and bruised. Once he lost consciousness and afterwards found himself in a closet lying on a stone floor. After this in a semi-conscious state, he felt himself taken up and carried away and then he found himself in the Red Crescent Hospital in bed. The man who had done so much to save the sick from the camps was a friend of his and in some way secured his release. When he was nearly well he sent him to us and we afterwards sent him to the consulate. One night, some weeks later we received a communication from Harpoot saying that a certain Kurdish patriarch whom we knew from the Dersim would be at our gate a little after dark and for forty pounds Turkish would take anyone who wished to go to Dersim. After dark I went to the consulate and brought the professor. We sent them off dressed as Kurds together with four or five other men. Then began a sort of underground railway for which our back porch was a station sending people to Dersim. But we stopped assisting in this work as soon as we felt it was no longer a matter of life and death. This method of escape went on for one and a half years, hundreds escaping until the Vali was changed in March, 1917. Then it all stopped.

At the time when people were taken from our hospital it was no longer possible to order people out from their homes and send them away. They would hide. Then the police began snapping them up wherever they found them, men, women and children, putting them in prison and sending them out. One day such a crowd was sent out and being weak they were only sent about two hours. One boy came back to us with about a dozen hacks and cuts from a hatchet on his back and head, and a bullet in his lung. He had been left for dead, but had crawled out and found his way to us. We had many such patients; one woman with a bullet in her jaw, one little girl with her neck cut. She said they had been laid one on top of another and their heads cut off two at a time. She was underneath, so her neck was not cut through. One woman fell, and feigned death, then afterwards found some of her children cut to pieces, others she did not find, but afterwards was always looking for them, hoping that they had escaped. One man from a village who was sent out in the beginning was tied up by one leg and whirled about with his head downward, then sent out and stabbed in the abdomen and then buried. He dug himself out and came to us and told us the story. He afterwards escaped to the Dersim.

One night a wounded police was brought in to us and he told me this story: A party of eleven Armenian men had escaped from a village which had been emptied. Police came to open the house of the village to put in the Moslem refugees from the Russian front. When they opened this house these men fired on them. Two or three from both sides were killed and wounded. Then the police set fire to the house and burned it, killing them as they came out. But this police told me that before he was shot he had killed the father and brother of the Armenian girl he had taken as his wife. I asked him how he could do such an awful thing. He replied that he had been ordered to do it and if he hadn't obeyed he would have been killed himself.

I heard one day that the thirteen year old daughter of Professor Vorperian had been brought back by a Turkish officer. The professor had been in our hospital in the beginning of the trouble, and had not been put in prison but was allowed to go with his family. This daughter told me the following story: They left Mezereh July 3, in the second crowd that was deported. They traveled together to Malatia two days' distance, though they were ten days in making the journey. This officer had kept close to their cart all the way. The parents noticed this and as the girl had very beautiful hair which they thought to be the attraction they cut it off; but the officer came to them and said that he wanted the girl and that it had been ordered that all the men should be killed, but if they would give him this girl he would save the father. This the professor refused to do, saying he would rather die and have her die with him. In Malatia the professor and his sixteen year old son were put into prison. Then the officer came to the mother; she gave the girl and the son was released from prison, but the father was taken out with the other men and was never heard of again. The officer brought the girl back to Mezereh and the mother and the other children came back later and lived with her. The girl told me that most of the women in the company were sent out from Malatia and a few girls who were brought back from their number said that the women, too, had been killed. Some girls brought back in this way became Moslems, but some were allowed to keep their own religion.

Pastor Vartan came to our hospital in the beginning of the troubles for an operation. We kept him sick as long as we could, but when the police came to take the Armenians Dr. Atkinson wrote him as a hospital servant in order to save him. The Kaimakam in Harpoot, though such a wicked man, for some reason, seemed willing to spare him and his family. His family had been left when the others were sent from Harpoot. When the Kaimakam learned the pastor was considered a hospital servant he wrote a letter to the Vali saying that this woman's husband was a servant in the hospital and asking that she be permitted to take a house and remain. Then he sent his servant with her and told her to get me to go with her and present this letter to the Vali. I was afraid to take her out on the street at that time for they were trying to make a clean sweep and were taking every Armenian to prison that could be found. But I was afraid that if she did not go it would anger the Kaimakam with her and he would withdraw the protection he had been giving to her. I had often gone out with the Armenians when they were afraid to go alone, and had never had anyone taken away from me on the street. So, after talking it over with Dr. Atkinson, I went. On the way the man with us was twice stopped by the police and questioned. I began to be afraid for her. Once we passed a group of Turkish men. I heard one of them say, "That also is an Armenian." When we reached the government building a Turk that I knew called me aside and asked me in a whisper if she were not an Armenian. The Commandant who was acting Vali at that time was not there. We were told to go to his office which was across town. We started and on the street we met a crowd of several hundred people from

Husenik, all that remained of that village, women and children and a few old men. They were being driven along through the street to prison. When they saw me they began to rush to me, begging for help, wanting me to take their children or to save their daughters. It was terrible to see. We took our stand at one side of the street and let them pass. One girl, a graduate from our college, then a teacher, a girl whom I had known and helped from the time she was a little girl, caught my hand and said in English, "Oh, why didn't you save me?" A police took his stand just behind me. He said nothing but I knew why he was there. I could do nothing, but I trembled for the woman beside me. They passed on and were sent out the next day. We went to the Commandant and he told me that the fate of the hospital workers had not yet been decided, so we went home. Two days later came Bayram, the Turkish festival and the deportations stopped, but we were not allowed to breathe freely.

One day a little later, the hospital was surrounded and all the workers were told to go to the police station and register. There was in the hospital then one woman from a wealthy family who had escaped from Malatia and returned. Police were hunting her to send her again as they feared she might later claim her property. Of course, we feared that they would send all of our servants and we had nearly a hundred at that time, although our patients were only about a hundred. The work had been divided and subdivided and each one had some kind of work. The Doctor, Miss Campbell and I all went to the police station with them. I was much afraid for this wealthy woman. I whispered to her asking her if she could sew and telling her she could register as our sewing woman. She did so, giving her name and place of residence exactly right and was not recognized, although we learned afterwards that the chief object of registering them all was to find her. After this we had about two months of comparative quiet. On November 4, Doctor had taken the children and gone to Harpoot. Two of our men were out burying a body, when suddenly the hospital was surrounded by police and no one could go out or come in, and those who were out were taken up and sent to the police station. I wanted to see what it meant. I ran to the gate but was not allowed to pass. I ran to another and was again sent back. Then I ran to another and told the guard there that he did not know his orders. That the Chief of Police would never refuse to let me go where I pleased and that if he didn't let me pass, I would report him. He looked ashamed and I laughed at him and he let me go. I found the streets in confusion, people crying everywhere, police running and groups of people gathered in places guarded by one or two men waiting to be taken to the police station. I ran to the police station and there crowds were being brought in. I asked for the Chief of Police. They said he was out and would not be in till sundown. A number of our own people were already there. I could do nothing till he came in. I started up another street and met a crowd of our own people being driven along. I also met some of the German missionary ladies. I told them we could do nothing till the Chief of Police came in and that he would not be in till sundown. "No," said one of the ladies, "he will not be in soon, he is out now riding like hell," and she did not mean to be profane. In a minute we saw him go tearing by on his back horse, riding just as she had said. On my way home, a window in the house of a Turkish officer was opened and four of our girls called to me that they had gone in there for refuge. I told them I would come for them after dark. When I reached home Doctor and the children had arrived. When the trouble began a little boy had run out to where the men were burying the woman and told them. They left the body on the stretcher and ran up to Harpoot to tell Dr. Atkinson. Nothing had happened up there as yet, so he came home as quickly as he could. The next morning we made out lists of all the people that we could claim and all their relatives and went to the Chief of Police and asked for them. The Germans did the same. It happened that we met before the women's prison. Their names were shouted at the door of the prison and one by one they came out. Just across the street was a mosque decorated with the German and Turkish flags and Moslems were going in to give thanks to God for the subjugation of Serbia and the opening of the Balkan railway. While we stood there two crowds of women and children from the villages were driven past. There must have been three or four hundred in each crowd. Such crowds usually appealed to us for help, but these passed in perfect silence, their heads bowed in dumb despair. At last our lists were finished. They had given us every one that we had asked for and we started away and the doors were closed. Then the wail that went up from those who were left behind I shall never forget. Why had not our faith been stronger when we presented our lists? Why had we not asked for more?

Late in the summer they quit putting the crowds that came from the north into the open camp, but shut them in the Gregorian cemetery which was enclosed with high walls. One day we heard that there were people there from Trebizond. Dr. Parmelee wanted to find some friends so I went with her down there. A large crowd had been sent out the night before, leaving only the weak, sick and dying. But there must have been several hundred of them. Bread was given to them, but not enough. They were dying from hunger and disease. A group of soldiers had dug a great big grave as big as a room and some six feet deep. When the people died their friends would climb down into the grave and put their bodies in until they had a layer all over the ground. Then a layer of dirt was thrown on. When I saw it one layer had been finished and another begun and the soldiers stood there leaning on their shovels, smoking their cigarettes and joking with each other. As I look back it seems terrible that there was no way of escape, but at the time I only thought of how glad I was that they could be buried in a cemetery instead of being left for the birds and the beasts, and that they could die quietly and not be killed.

About the end of October Dr. Atkinson took a trip around Lake Guljuk, which was about fifteen miles distant. He had only gone a short distance when he began to see bodies by the roadside. Near the foot of the mountain were a great number, these still having their clothes on. But around the lake he estimated that there were between five and ten thousand all entirely naked, nearly all women and children and nearly all of the women showed signs of mutilation, let us hope after death. They showed signs of having been killed in various ways. Some were shot, some beheaded, many were hacked or cut with hatchets or knives. This doubtless done by Kurds rather than soldiers. In one place he found a ravine where the bodies lay four or five deep just as they had fallen. They had evidently been stripped and then crowded over the precipice. In some places, the Kurds who lived in the neighborhood had evidently tried to rid themselves of the stench by gathering the bodies together and burning them. These evidently were not our own people, but were from the regions north of us, as was indicated by many papers that were found scattered about. In the valley where the Americans usually camp at the Lake, there was nothing at all. These people were without doubt some of the thousands who had camped outside Mezereh during the summer. Is it any wonder that Dr. Atkinson came home sick at heart, not wanting to live any longer on this wicked earth?

Two months later he died and I was left to face life without him, yet not alone, for God's presence and power were wonderful in those days. The very men who had given us so much trouble, those whose hands were red with human blood, came to grasp my hand and weep over him.

At the time the doctor died we had 65 Armenians registered as hospital workers. We had three houses rented in Mezereh. One filled with the children of our workers. During the deportations we had kept 35 of these children in the big, clean operating room which we were not using at that time. Two other houses were filled with people whom we had rescued but who were homeless. We had also sent many up to Harpoot. The great weight that rested on me at the time of his death was the Armenians. When we had had such a hard time when working together to save them, what could I do alone? But God lifted this weight in a certain assurance which came to me that nothing more would happen to them. Miss McLaren came to us at that time from Van, and I shall always think she was sent directly by God. She was a great help and comfort to me. The officials were usually kind to me and I was rarely refused when I asked a favor of them. Once or twice lower officials tried to impose upon me. The higher officials always took my part when I appealed to them. My one desire was to hold onto the hospital till my husband's successor could come at the end of the war. In April the Red Cross funds were cut off and we could no longer support the Turkish soldiers in the hospital. But we offered to keep them and still care for them, the government furnishing their food. They seemed glad to have us do this and still left the hospital in our hands. We were given one of the remaining Armenian doctors to look after the patients, and later on we were given a German surgeon and when he left, a Greek.

When news of the breaking of relations with America came, we had in the hospital about 125 Turkish soldiers, 25 or 30 private patients, mostly poor, whom we were supporting from the income from the pharmacy. We had always kept back a part of the hospital for our own patients. There were only about 16 Armenian servants and nurses, the others all having escaped to the Dersim. The Turkish doctors begged me to stay and promised me that every protection would be given me, even though war should be declared and that I might keep the control of the hospital in my own hands. It was hard to go and turn over the hospital which had been my husband's life work into the hands of the Turkish government. On the other hand, the Ambassador was urging us to go and it didn't seem right to remain with my three children when famine was staring us in the face. I decided to go. I turned the hospital over to the government with the understanding that they were holding it in trust to the end of the war. We made lists of everything belonging to the hospital, they and I signing them, they, both civil and military governments keeping a copy and I keeping one. Then I asked them to continue to let the income from the pharmacy support the poor sick, as I had been doing. They promised to do this. Then they decided to send all the soldiers out and open the hospital to the public. After I left a letter from our pharmacist told me that they were doing this and at that time had 70 or 80 patients in the hospital, nearly all poor Armenians, and that they were all clean and well cared for. All the Armenian servants I had left were still there. I could ask no more than this.

I feel that I know the wickedness of the Turk pretty well, but my heart's desire for him is that he may be saved, saved from his power over other nationalities, but most of all saved from himself. I want him to lose his power to rule, even himself, until he can learn how to do it. I want him made powerless to forbid the light of the Gospel to his own people. I want the way to be opened for a band of men and women to go in and teach the gospel of love and mercy. I want the Moslem world to be saved for Christ. If God permits, I want to be one of those to go, for I love Turkey and the Turk.

[Signed] Tacy W. Atkinson

ADVERTISEMENT

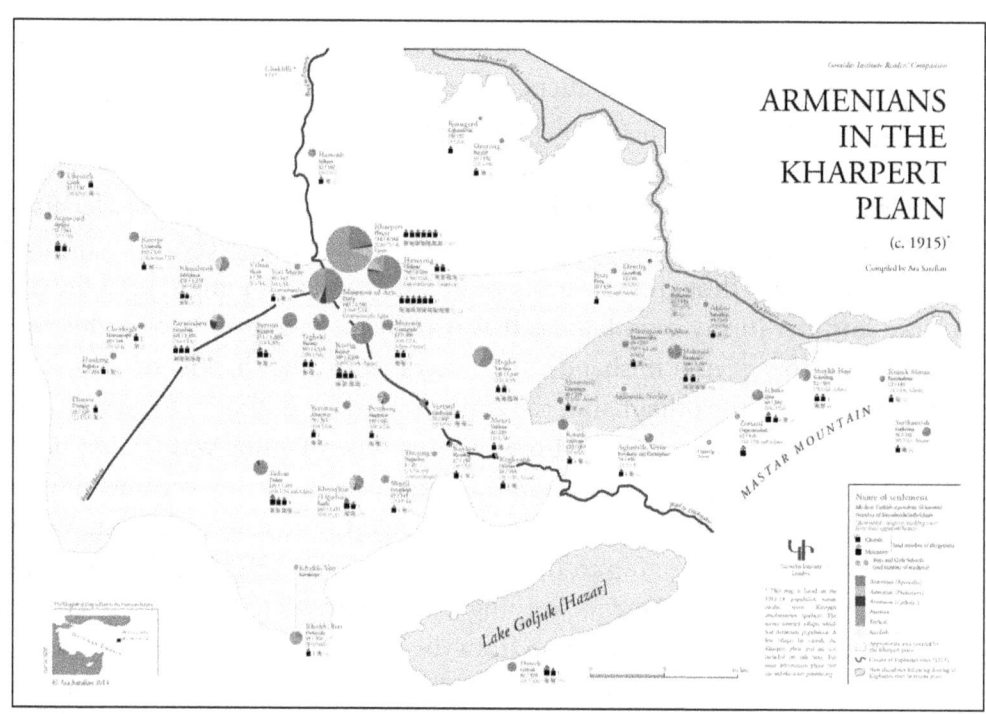

Gomidas Institute Readers' Companion Series

"Armenians in the Kharpert Plain" circa. 1915

Large format (23 x 16 niches), detailed, color map, printed on heavy paper.
US$10.00 / UK£8.00
To order please email *books@gomidas.org*

Glossary

Araba = Cart
Arachnort (*Arm.*) = Armenian prelate, community leader
Baron, Brn. (*Arm.*) = Mr.
Bayram = A Muslim religious festival
Buyurlty = Official travel permit
Chantas = Bag, case, pouch
Chaoush = Seargeant
Charshaf = Women's outdoor overgarment
Chiftlik = Farm
Dellal = Town crier
Digin (*Arm.*) = Mrs.
Doshek = Mattress
Firman = Imperial edict, command
Furar = Deserter
Goel, ghul = Lake
Hammal = Porter
Hanum = Mrs.
Inshaat = Construction
Kaimakam = Mayor, head official of a district
Katur, Katurjis = Mule, Muleteer
Kavass = Consular guard
Khan = Inn
Kuzzlebash = Member of the (Muslim) Alevi sect
Merkez = Center
Mudir = Public official, administrator
Mutassarif = Governor of a sub-province
Nefer = Private soldier
Pilav = A rice dish
Pompish = Title given to a Protestant pastor's wife
Ramazan = A Muslim religious festival of fasting
Red Konak = Name of government house in Mezreh
Salaam = Greeting of peace

www.ingramcontent.com/pod-product-compliance
Lightning Source LLC
Chambersburg PA
CBHW080551170426
43195CB00016B/2757